SAINTS
and
SWINGERS

By William P. Barker

As Matthew Saw the Master
Everyone in the Bible
They Stood Boldly
Who's Who in Church History
Saints and Swingers

The Under-Thirties in the Bible

SAINTS
and
SWINGERS

William P. Barker

Fleming H. Revell Company
Old Tappan, New Jersey

Scripture quotes in the volume are from the *Revised Standard Version of the Bible, Copyright 1946 and 1952,* unless otherwise identified.

Scripture quotes identified TEV are from the Today's English Version of the New Testament. Copyright © American Bible Society 1966.

Scripture quotations identified NEB are from *The New English Bible.* © The Delegates of the Oxford University Press and the Syndics of the Cambridge University Press 1961, 1970. Reprinted by permission.

Excerpt from *Death of a Salesman* by Arthur Miller published by The Viking Press, Inc. is used by permission.

Excerpt from *Tea and Sympathy* by Robert Anderson published by Random House, Inc. © 1954 is used by permission.

SBN 8007-0446-0 Cloth
SBN 8007-0459-2 Paper

TO
the members of
Calvary Presbyterian Church, Canton, Ohio

Contents

Preface

DOES THE BIBLE have any meaning to those growing up in the psychedelic seventies? Can the Age of Abraham speak to the Age of Aquarius? Does He who bore the love beam up Calvary say anything to those who wear love beads on Carnaby Street?

The thesis of this book is to answer these questions with an emphatic *yes!* Jesus Christ's life, death and resurrection are still the pivotal events in the history of every under-thirty person as well as over. The character studies of some of the under-thirties in the Bible are both exposition and examples of that thesis.

Every author knows that every book is actually the product of many, many persons whose insights and assistance help make it a reality. Special recognition, therefore, must be given to many of the under-thirty group who shared their ideas so generously and who gave me so many new glimpses into the meaning of the Good News: my own college-age children, John and Ellen, the students at Pittsburgh Theological Seminary, and young people at numerous retreats, conferences and campuses where I have been privileged to serve.

Appreciation must also be expressed to the New Wilmington Missionary Conference where many of these chapters were presented as lectures; to Fred M. Rogers and the Luxor Ministerial Association for countless ideas; to Mrs. D. Wayne Fraker for typing and proofreading the manuscript; and to Jean for her unflagging wifely encouragement.

WILLIAM P. BARKER

SAINTS
and
SWINGERS

1

The Hippy

THE YOUNG MAN had chosen to slip into the subculture of rootless, restless drifters. His wanderings and his life style, he assured himself, were the price to be paid for being so different from everyone back home.

Why had he left? They were all such stupid squares, he asserted. He excoriated his family and hometown. Couldn't stomach their hypocrisy and dullness, he proclaimed angrily. Denouncing their piety and values, he added that he had been pushed out, forced to turn his back on that kind of a degenerate society.

The young man bristled with hostilities. For all his protestations of peace and innocence, he exhibited little love. His very name, Cain, meaning *'spear,'* seemed to convey something of his sinister, destructive streak.

Occasionally Cain remembered that, true to his name, he had once literally used a spear on his kid brother, Abel.

Cain had loathed Abel. Even when Cain had once been part of the straight world of haircuts, button-down collars and 9 to 5 jobs, he had despised Abel.

Abel, Cain told himself, had always been such a nuisance and clod. All that Abel ever seemed to think about was sheep and God. Spent all of his time with those stupid sheep. In fact, Cain thought, Abel hung around those silly sheep so much that he seemed to

become sheeplike himself. Dumb, dull Abel. My own sheep-y
brother. Abel even smelled like a sheep, he'd been around them
so much, Cain recalled. How many times had Cain told the kid to
bathe and clean up before he came around. Abel never seemed to
get anything through that thick sheep head of his. And Abel would
keep turning up at embarrassing times. Cain angrily remembered
how he would have to drag along little Abel when they were both
boys. "Be sure to look after Abel, son," old man Adam, their
father, used to tell Cain. Cain reminisced that he had been sick
and tired of the whole family even as a child.

Cain had been the bright, active brother. Cain the spear: sharp,
direct and dangerous. "You'll never find me meandering around
on hillsides with a flock!" Cain told everyone. "I'm going to make
it big! And I'm going to enjoy the easy life. There's no future in
sheep. It's in marketing, in knowing how to wheel and deal. Let
others stand out in the rain with sheep, not me!"

Cain smiled grimly, remembering his days as the successful
young businessman. He had used his land to farm. He had got a
good price on his grain. Cannily using his profits to buy more
fields, Cain had built up his acreage.

He hired others to do the hard work, assuming a supervisory
role for himself. With youthful pride, he had the words THE CAIN
FARMS, lettered on all the equipment and implements. Instead of
walking out to work and laboring all day in the sun himself, Cain
rode around each morning in the cool of the day, inspecting things
and returning to his comfortable home before it got too hot. No
crick in *his* back from hoeing, he told himself; no sore arms or
blisters from plowing and threshing for him. No sir! Hired hands
got the tired backs and sore arms, not Cain. With their sunburned
necks and dirty fingernails, Cain smugly noted, the hired men
(*"my* men") took off their hats as he rode up. It was, "Good
morning, Mr. Cain," and, "Nice day, Mr. Cain." Cain enjoyed
the deference from men old enough to be his father.

Cain recalled that he had dreamed of expanding. Instead of The
Cain Farms, it would be Cain Enterprises, Incorporated. Of course
it would take more land. The nearest and best acreage, however,
was being used by Abel. All that pasture for those sheep of Abel's,

Cain had noted, could have been turned into high-yield investment for Cain. When Cain had suggested working out some sort of a deal, Abel had said that he just wanted to go on with his shepherd work. Stupid Abel and his dumb sheep again, Cain thought. How Cain had loathed his brother!

It was easy for Cain to recollect what led up to the last time he had to put up with Abel. It was the session of the big religious festival. Everyone was expected to bring an offering.

Abel had brought his prize ewe. How stupid of Abel, Cain had thought. When Abel could have brought some worn-out old ram, he had brought the best of his flock. What a dummy, letting his faith cost him so much, Cain had mused. Abel never seemed to wise up and learn the shortcuts.

Cain had grudgingly chipped in something from the surplus in one of the enormous storage bins on The Cain Farms. He knew that he had to keep up appearances. At the same time, he was tired of conforming to the pressures to give so much so frequently. All this worship twaddle got in the way of business. And if everyone had wanted to get down to cases, Cain figured, his gift from The Cain Farms was worth a lot more than that one sheep of Abel's. Anyone could tell that Cain was the real giver. His offering, Cain told himself, would obviously carry a lot more weight with the Almighty than Abel's.

To his intense disgust, Cain noticed that Abel's offering was accepted as the better gift! Angrily, he stormed into the Lord's presence and demanded an explanation.

"If you do well, will you not be accepted?" (Genesis 4:7) replied the Lord. In other words, the Lord was interested in more than impressive gifts and elaborate ritual. Faithfulness to Him in the everyday acts and attitudes was what made worship acceptable.

Cain had not understood that the gates of acceptance were still open and that he was not rejected forever. He only knew that God preferred Abel's offering.

Cain's anger had prevented him from remembering the rest of the conversation with the Lord. Cain had not listened to the warning, ". . . if you do not well, sin is couching at the door; its desire is for you, but you must master it" (4:7). Storming out of the presence of the Lord, Cain had muttered that had it not been for Abel his brother, his own offering would have been accepted.

Cain, infuriated with Abel, had remembered all the occasions in which Abel had interfered with Cain's plans or Cain's pleasures. I've put up with that contemptible bit of scum for long enough. I've had it! He has got to go, Cain had raged within himself.

Cain could recall the details of the plot as vividly as the day in which the deed was done. He had invited Abel over to The Cain Farms. After making sure that no one would be around as witness, Cain took the unsuspecting brother for a walk to a remote field. Suddenly, without warning, Cain speared Abel. As his brother's lifeblood soaked into the earth, Cain hastily dug a shallow grave. He looked around. Noting that he was unobserved, Cain pushed Abel's still-warm corpse into the hole, covered it with dirt and arranged the site to look part of the recently-plowed field. No one would ever know, Cain smugly assured himself. At last he was free of the obnoxious Abel.

Cain the wanderer still rankled when he remembered that God had detected that Abel was missing. Cain recalled how irked he had been by God's question, "Where is Abel your brother" (4:9)? Cain still wondered why the Lord insisted on checking up on good-for nothing Abel. The Lord, Cain had noticed, had not inquired about Cain, but about his stupid kid brother. Why did God keep dragging in Abel all the time? Cain fumed.

After all, he reasoned, religion is a private matter. Strictly between me and the Lord. Just us—two is company, three's a crowd. I don't want my brother getting in the way and messing things up when it comes to religion.

Cain never could understand that responsibility to God is responsibility for one's brother! No person is permitted the privilege of private interviews with the Almighty; as a matter of fact, audiences are granted only when a person brings his brother's needs to God before he presents his own! "Where is Abel your brother?" God asks before He will discuss Cain.

God had asked Cain a direct question, "Where is Abel?" Although Cain insisted on denying it, Cain lied to the Lord, ". . . I do not know . . ." (4:9). Cain *did* know. As if this were not enough, Cain insulted the Lord, sarcastically adding, "Am I my brother's keeper" (4:9)? "Do I have to play shepherd to the Shepherd?" Cain snapped; "Why should I have to give an account of myself regarding my brother's welfare?"

God, impatient with the impertinent Cain, roared, "What have you done" (4:10)? Who did Cain think He was, usurping Divine prerogatives of giving and taking life? Did this young man, Cain, forget that blood and life belong to the Lord of all existence? Why had Cain presumed to attack and destroy what belonged to God? How could he dare to hold cheaply and to terminate the breath-puff (the literal meaning of the name Abel) for whom he had a special brotherly responsibility?

God then told young Cain that there was no permanent place in His realm for a man who refused to be responsible for others. There would never be contentment or security for Cain, God assured the young murderer. ". . . you shall be a fugitive and wanderer on the earth . . ." (4:12) the Lord stated.

Cain had shrugged. If this was the way that he was going to be talked to by the Chief, Cain decided that he would just as soon clear out. Cain told himself that he did not have to take this kind of treatment from anybody, not even God.

Only one thing worried Cain. Suppose someone should murder *him?* Who would avenge his death? Who would even care if he lived or died? As a fugitive and wanderer, Cain knew that he'd be fair prey for everyone. Cain began to sense how desperately alone he would be.

Cain complained to God. God had driven him away, Cain whined, and he'd be hidden from God's face, forgetting that earlier he had tried to hide his real self from God! ". . . whoever finds me will slay me" (4:14) sniffled the man who had schemed to slay his own brother.

God still cared. He promised Cain *His* protection. The Lord assured Cain that He would be Cain's next of kin, promising Cain that if anyone took Cain's life, He, the Lord, would take up the family responsibilities of avenging Cain's death! God generously granted to Cain what Cain had refused to do for his own brother, Abel. As a sign of His pledge of protection, God placed a mark on Cain's forehead.

"Then Cain went away from the presence of the Lord . . ." (4:16). Although marked with a promise, the sullen young man stalked out and headed east. He cynically assured himself that promises are flimsy. Negative and angry toward everyone connected with home, Cain vowed that he would never have anything to do with God or God's family again.

Cain ". . . dwelt in the land of Nod . . ." (4:16). *Nod* is the word for "fugitive"; Cain, in other words, existed in a state of restlessness. Unable to be at home anywhere, the world's first hippy began his uneasy, fitful wanderings, vainly imagining that the way of repudiation would somehow be the means of release.

Restless wanderers though we may be, we carry both the mark of Cain and the mark of Christ. Through Him who was pitted with nail holes, we are marked with love! God's promise to us is that although we may sink forgotten into the ground, whether murdered or murderer, we are remembered by Him.

2
The Tough-Breaks Kid

THE BOY was grabbed from behind. Although only seventeen, he fought with the strength of a man. He knew, however, that there were too many of them. He tried to struggle free and run.

In spite of his desperate battle, he was overpowered and flung to the ground. Powerful arms trussed him with rope until his arms were tightly lashed. Still squirming violently, he found himself being dragged along the rocky ground. Suddenly, he saw what was going to happen. Before him was a dark hole—the mouth of a deep cistern. He guessed that he would be dumped into that cistern. Visions of drowning in the dark depths flashed through his mind. He jerked and heaved, frantically trying to escape. Seconds later, he felt himself dropping.

He screamed in terror. Abruptly, his plunge ended. The boy found himself lying in wet mud at the bottom of the deep hole. He spat out a mouthful of the oozy slime and twisted his aching body in the slippery muck so that he could see the circle of daylight above. As he lay panting, he grimly started to plan how he would report this episode to his father when he got home.

His assailants were his own half-brothers. Angrily, the boy remembered the long series of skirmishes with them. He knew that they hated him. If tying him up and dumping him in the cistern was their idea of a practical joke, he'd show them.

19

He had shown them before, he recalled with satisfaction. In fact, he had always shown them up. Even as a child, he had shown them up by being the one son in the family who had received a fancy, long-sleeved coat. He remembered smugly that he had always been his father's favorite. His brothers had always said that their father had spoiled him. True, the boy had to admit to himself, he sometimes showed some obnoxious characteristics, such as tattling on his older brothers. How they resented him!

As the boy lay in the deep, dark pit, he thought again how he had shown up the brothers with his dreams. Those dreams had infuriated them, he remembered. One dream depicted eleven sheaves of grain bowing to a more prominent sheaf. His eleven brothers had caught the obvious symbolism and had reacted angrily. Another dream, which had annoyed even his permissive, easygoing father, portrayed eleven stars plus the sun and moon circling obsequiously around the boy's star.

From the depths of the pit, the boy heard his brothers' voices. He strained to catch their words. It was obvious that they were discussing him.

"Let's kill Joseph!" one of the brothers growled. Another concurred. "Yeah, kill him." A murmur of approval followed.

The boy gasped. Killed? Brotherly squabbles were one thing. Fratricide was entirely different. Joseph was unprepared for a murder plot. And by his own brothers!

Bitterly, he told himself that he never would have made the three-day errand for his father if he had known that he was going to be killed by his brothers. Although Joseph knew that they detested him as a precocious brat, he never, never, had suspected that they would stoop to murder. Somehow, being his blood relatives, he had expected more of them. Joseph felt tears coming to his eyes. The pain of disappointment in his brothers almost matched the terror he felt.

Joseph waited for them to seal the hole of the cistern with a slab and depart. It was useless to shout or scream, because no one would hear or care. He wondered how long he would survive. The darkness, the hunger, and the thirst would eventually get him, he knew. It was easy to imagine the stomach pains, the progressing debilitation, the eventual lassitude and the final coma as the days would go by without food or water. Days? Joseph wondered how in the darkness he would even be able to measure the passing of time—as if it would matter when he was entombed alive in a pit.

What were his brothers still discussing? Joseph wondered. Straining to hear, he heard fragments of sentences about a caravan—and there were other voices. Joseph listened as his brothers haggled with desert nomads from a caravan over the price of a slave.

It became apparent to Joseph that he was the slave. His own brothers now planned to sell him to the traders. He shuddered. If he got hauled out of the cistern and turned over to slave-dealers, Joseph knew it would be merely swapping one form of death for another. Either way, it was certain that he would be extinct. Slavery was a living death. Joseph remembered the stories of the unspeakable cruelties often practiced on slaves—of the killing marches without adequate food or water, shackled behind an animal for weeks on end, in scorching desert heat. Joseph also knew that he would be separated permanently from his home. Slaves, as common chattel, never returned to parents, friends, or childhood scenes.

Joseph saw a rope with a noose lowered. He felt the noose settle over his torso and tighten. A moment later, hauled to the surface like a grain sack, Joseph lay on the ground, blinking in the bright daylight.

A couple of his brothers were counting the silver coins paid for Joseph. Joseph could tell that they were congratulating themselves over the way they had managed to get him off their hands for keeps and make a good profit. Others were butchering a sheep, preparing to smear the blood over Joseph's garments before returning home. They were laughing about the story they were concocting—that a wild animal had torn him apart. So this was the way they would explain his absence at home, Joseph observed.

Tethered like an animal behind the caravan, he plodded silently away. The next weeks stretched into a nearly-unbearable ordeal of trying to survive in the searing heat and swirling dust. When the caravan finally hobbled into Egypt, Joseph's hopes sank lower. Wearily, the boy stumbled into the slave mart, where he was peddled like a bit of merchandise.

Life, Joseph discovered, could apparently be absurd and meaningless. His future agenda, it seemed, would list only loneliness and injustice. Joseph mused about the purpose of human existence. What's it all about? Where does it all end? Is oblivion the summary of a man's personal dossier, death and concluding absurdity? Why make the effort to survive?

Like a subliminal slogan repeatedly flickering on a screen for a split second, almost unseen yet always remembered, Joseph's biographer inserts a phrase which flashes throughout the story of young Joseph's troubles: "The Lord was with Joseph . . ." (Genesis 39:2, 21). Joseph, the one-time brash braggart, suffered a series of raw deals, but never soured into embittered cynicism. Not with the Lord who promised His presence with him in the pit, in the slavetrain, in the strange culture and foreign land of Egypt!

Joseph was bought by a wealthy Egyptian government official named Potiphar. Joseph's integrity, industry and intelligence were so obvious that he quickly moved up through the ranks of Potiphar's household staff. Soon, Joseph was given additional responsibilities until he finally enjoyed such trust by Potiphar that the Hebrew slave boy found himself managing all the Egyptian owner's affairs.

Potiphar's wife also found Joseph interesting. Typical of Egyptian upper-crust society, she was vain and sensual, corrupt and bored. The woman eyed the virile-looking young Hebrew and had designs on him. She flashed all the usual messages that she was willing to have an affair with him. Surprised and miffed when she was ignored, the wife accelerated her campaign to seduce Joseph. She unblushingly offered herself.

The author of Genesis had no prudery about describing the scene. The thirty-ninth chapter is the ancient yet ever-contemporary situation of a lonely man away from home, a lonely woman who is not his wife but willing to go to bed with him for some attention.

Joseph was no unemotional mummy. He was a normal, red-blooded young man in his late teens. Flattered by the woman's advances, and acutely aware of his own male-ness, Joseph found himself enticed.

Why not? Who'll ever know? Nobody'll get hurt. Why not get what I can? I'm entitled to a little fun, too. Besides, everyone's doing it. And she asked me. She started it. I'm here in the city now, not back home where everyone knows me. I'm no longer a kid from a small town; I'm part of a different culture. When in Egypt do as the Egyptians. This is the day of the new morality. And I'm lonely. She understands. Maybe I'm more of a lover than I dared to think! Why not go ahead? It may even help my career. Besides, if anyone finds out, she'll shield me. It's really the easiest way out of the predicament. Go along. Just this once—don't be a prude.

The hardest word in any language is sometimes the simple word no! Joseph refused to go along with Potiphar's wife.

The plot is the same today, although the scenery and setting and cast may be slightly different. Many modern Josephs are asking Joseph's *Why not?* One is lonely, the other is willing. Both know that today most of the old reasons for sex morality—detection, infection or conception—are now removed.

". . . how then can I do this great wickedness," Joseph exclaimed, "and sin against God?" (39:9). Joseph was not squeamish about calling things by their proper title. Sleeping around was *sin* to Joseph, not "sowing a few wild oats" or "doing what comes naturally" or "following my drives" or "having a few kicks."

God, always on the scene, is in control of the human scene. For our good, He puts bounds on our lovemaking.

Joseph understood that he was accountable to God. He knew that he was not free to do as he pleased. He claimed no right to free love, but only to a mutually-responsible, permanent relationship with one other. Even sex, as Joseph indicated by his actions, is one of God's gifts but can be enjoyed only when, before God, a man and woman announce publicly that they will be committed to one another at every level for keeps.

Moreover, Joseph stated that he was accountable to others. Because God would not break faith with Joseph, Joseph would not break faith with the woman's husband, Potiphar. Nor would Joseph exploit the woman, regardless how anxious she was. He knew that each would be using the other. Having both her welfare and her husband's at heart, Joseph refused to take advantage of either the woman or her husband.

Joseph scrupulously avoided being caught in a compromising situation. Knowing the temptation of having an affair with the boss's wife, Joseph concocted excuses to keep from being alone in the house with her.

One day, however, Joseph discovered that Potiphar's wife schemed to catch him in the house when no one was around. He politely started to leave. Suddenly, he felt her clasping her arms around his body. He heard her seductively pleading.

Abruptly, Joseph broke away and started to flee.

The woman, however, clutched at Joseph's clothes, ripping a piece from his tunic as he twisted to escape her embrace. True to the saying, ". . . nor Hell a fury like a woman scorned," the spurned woman screamed and screamed. Unable to seduce Joseph, she hysterically shrieked that Joseph had tried to rape her!

Joseph was arrested. It was hopeless to try to explain, especially with the torn piece of his clothing as incriminating evidence. Who would believe him—a foreigner and slave? Joseph was imprisoned.

Virtue does not necessarily pay off. Responsibility can mean knocks. Joseph was neither the first nor the last to learn that trust in God is not hiring the Lord as personal bodyguard or buying a protection policy. Thirteen years of enduring the heat, flies, insults, dirt, brutality and confinement of an Egyptian jail made it clear that it does not always pay to be good.

Joseph had ample time to ponder. Although innocent, he had been handed another tough break. The young Hebrew's experiences in pit, slave gang and prison would have tempted him to curse in anger or despair at the apparently unreasonable order to existence. Life a grim sentence in one pit, relieved only by a permanent sentence to the final pit? Not to Joseph. For thirteen tedious years in jail, ". . . the Lord was with Joseph and showed him steadfast love . . . (39:21).

As another God-haunted man, also well acquainted with prisons, wrote some fifteen hundred years later, "I have the strength to face all conditions by the power that Christ gives to me" (Philippians 4:13; TEV). Paul the Apostle, along with a heroic host of God's jailbirds including John Bunyan, Samuel Rutherford and Dietrich Bonhoeffer, knew Joseph's secret. God's steadfast love sustains and empowers men even in the midst of injustice, intrigue and inhumanity!

3
The Playboy

SHE WAS ATTRACTIVE, and he wanted her. He took steps immediately to have her. It was as simple as that.

The young man was used to getting what he wanted. His name, Samson, could be translated roughly as "Sunshine" or "Sunny," hinting at the warmth and joy his arrival brought to his elderly parents who had been childless for many, many years. From his boyhood, Samson learned to cultivate a sunny winsomeness in keeping with his name. Undoubtedly, much of this sunshine-like personality came from being an only child and having his own way much of the time. Furthermore, he quickly developed into an enormous youngster, gifted with prodigious strength. Noting that his shoulders and height commanded respect even as a boy, Samson acquired the bright, jaunty air of one who can shove his way ahead.

His devout father and mother, grateful for a baby after years of wanting a child, dedicated young Samson to the Lord. A Nazarite (one consecrated to the Lord) was a man who permitted no iron tool such as a razor to touch his head, so Samson, as a Nazarite boy, grew a luxuriant plume of hair. He quickly noticed that his flowing mane as well as his physique served as an attention-getter. Later, as his beard developed into a great handsome bush, accenting his handsome features and powerful body, he gloried in never shaving or clipping his marvelous growth. Although Samson took pride in being a Nazarite, it was more out of personal vanity than from a spiritual commitment. His Nazarite vow gave him an excuse for preening himself as an exceptionally stylish, good-looking young man-about-town.

Samson quickly observed that he caught the eye of the girls. When he noticed a certain Philistine girl who seemed particularly interested in him, Samson made up his mind that he was going to enjoy her.

Playboy Samson, determined to have his affair, ignored the fact that she was a Philistine, and that any relationship with any Philistine was bound to mean trouble for an Israelite. The Philis-tines, with their superior military, technical, commercial and organizational skills, controlled everything. Samson's people had been bullied into submission by the Philistine troops, who carried *iron* swords and spears (the secret weapons which nobody else possessed at that time). Reduced to serving as vassals to the Philis-tine overlords, the people of Israel smarted under the humiliation, and fought a long series of bloody guerilla skirmishes. Samson, more interested in his conquest of the girl than in the Philistine forces, showed something less than the patriotism he should have felt.

Samson, however, convinced himself that he would outsmart the wily Philistines. Besides, if he wanted the woman, why shouldn't he have her? She's willing, Samson told himself. Why should anyone get all worked up about consequences?

Samson went to his father and, with the imperious tone of a boy who has been given everything he wanted, demanded, "Get her for me, for she pleases me well" (Judges 14:3).

It was customary for a father to arrange a son's marriage, in that culture. Samson's father, however, delayed carrying out Samson's request because it went against his wishes.

Headstrong Samson, disregarding his parent's ideas, took matters into his own hands. He impulsively arranged the marriage himself, anxious to complete his conquest. He was not going to be thwarted.

Furthermore, he knew that he could always turn on the sunny charm which always succeeded in warming any cool feelings toward him.

One day on one of his trips down to his girl's home at the Philistine village of Timnath before the wedding, Samson encountered a lion. Samson killed the animal with his bare hands, astonishing himself with his strength and increasing his cocky self-confidence. On his next visit, Samson noticed some bees building a hive in the carcass of the dead lion.

He should have suspected that the wedding festivities would not proceed smoothly when he observed that apart from his father, all the guests were Philistine friends of the bride's family. Samson felt that the Philistine wedding guests were inclined to dismiss him as a big, uncouth hillbilly. He thought to himself, I'll show these Philistines that I'm no yokel, but just as smart as they are—if not a bit smarter! Remembering the honeybees in the lion's body, Samson planned a riddle to stump the guests. He cunningly decided to add some excitement by making a heavy bet that no one in the group would be able to guess the answer within a week.

The guests, who knew they'd be considered poor sports if they refused Samson's wager, accepted. Then they heard the riddle: "Out of the eater came something to eat. Out of the strong came something sweet." Try as they did, the Philistine men could not guess the answer. While Samson strutted with pride, anticipating a big pay-off on his bets, the surly Philistines began to plot. They finally went to Samson's bride-to-be and threatened her life if she would not wheedle the answer from Samson and tell them.

Samson, seeing his bride's tears, allowed himself to be gulled into giving her the answer. Not long afterward, he was enraged to hear his new Philistine in-laws chant the answer to his riddle. Samson stomped out in a huff, and went on a rampage against some Philistines at Ashkelon to collect enough loot to pay off his bets. Still boiling with anger, Samson returned to his parents' home. He did not even think about the bride he had left in the Philistine village.

Samson finally remembered the girl. At least, he told himself, I'm supposed to have her for my wife, so I'll go down and have some fun. He took a present, scheming to get her into her bedroom with him as quickly as possible.

The girl's family, facing disgrace because she had not been married to Samson after all the celebration and hullabaloo earlier, had meanwhile hurriedly wed her to the best man! When the father broke this news to the brideless groom, Samson exploded in another tantrum.

Samson, who childishily threw his weight around and pushed things over when he did not get his own way, seethed and sulked, If I cannot have the woman I want, I'll make them sorry. Somehow, he rounded up three hundred foxes. After tying them by the tails into pairs, he attached a lighted torch to each pair and turned them loose in the Philistines' grain fields. The destruction of fields and orchards was staggering.

Clever though the exploit was, it was a stunt. It was not part of a campaign against a grim and tenacious enemy. Loosing foxes with firebrands was in the category of a practical joke, not carefully-planned tactics devised to help achieve the Israelite goal of shaking off the Philistine yoke.

Samson seemed surprised when the Philistines retaliated by burning alive the girl and her family. An undisciplined but powerful one-man army, he furiously roamed through the Philistine valleys in a bloody orgy of revenge.

Samson's escapades propelled him to leadership among the confederation of tribes of Israel. As a judge or chief, the muscular young Nazarite led a series of impromptu raids—never a well-planned campaign calculated to win permanent victory—to stave off the repeated threats of the Philistines. Some of Samson's strongman displays became legends, such as the time he single-handedly carried off the city gates of Gaza one night to escape capture; or the occasion he, a prisoner, burst his ropes, seizing the only object nearby suitable as a weapon, an ass's jawbone, laid low an entire Philistine army!

Although "the Spirit of the Lord came mightily upon him" (Judges 14:19; 15:14) during many of his feats, Samson's thoughts were more on girls than on God. The man who might have been used by Israel's God to lead his nation to a series of superb victories dissipated his energies on a string of boudoir conquests. The real enemy for Samson, as Samson himself at times half-suspected, was not the Philistines but his own passions.

He felt little responsibility to others and convinced himself that life's meaning consisted in gratifying his sex desires. His first marriage had fizzled because Samson had confused lust with love. Dismayingly, Samson persuaded himself that he did not even need to go through the pretense of a wedding in his playboy career. Pathetically unwilling to commit himself permanently to one woman, he rushed from one girl to another. Samson unwittingly found himself unable to have a meaningful relationship with another woman. A girl for him was merely a sex object. When playboy Samson discovered that few women choose to be used as mere toys for a man's gratification, he resorted to buying his pleasure for the evening.

Anything goes, and even if I hunt up a call girl, I'm going to enjoy myself in any case. Marriage only would spoil things. Besides, I'm the champ! I'm the mighty Samson! I can do as I please. All those old-fashioned rules don't hold anymore. This is a new day. Forget all those prissy puritan hang-ups. The world would be a lot happier, if everyone would express themselves and stop being so repressed!

Samson, growing increasingly sensual and slothful, eventually drifted into a sordid affair with a girl named Delilah. Delilah knew Samson's reputation. She shrewdly guessed that Samson would hang around only as long as he got what he wanted. When Philistine agents offered her fat bribes to ferret out the secret of Samson's incredible physical strength, Delilah decided to play both Samson and the Philistines for all they were worth.

Samson, infatuated with Delilah, made her his mistress. Unconcerned about any future ramifications of their relationship, he treated her as a tool for the present's pleasure. Even when Delilah began to crossexamine him pointedly and repeatedly about the source of his phenomenal power, Samson ignored the warning signs, telling himself: As long as she'll sleep with me, why worry?

When the Philistines began pressing Delilah to coax Samson's secret so they could seize him, Delilah resorted to using all the wiles she had. She pleaded. She pouted. She cried. Samson jokingly told her one night that if he were tied up with seven fresh, wet bowstrings, he'd be as helpless as anyone else. Waking after a bout of lovemaking, Samson discovered that she had bound him with seven such bowstrings. After popping the bowstrings, he laughed, instead of wising up.

Delilah pretended to be hurt, and cried, claiming that Samson was mocking her by not telling him how he could be overpowered. Eager to stop the tears and have her amuse him again with her caresses, Samson hastily concocted the story that he'd be helpless if trussed up in brand-new rope. He was startled to have her wake him shouting, "The Philistines are upon you, Samson!" and to feel heavy ropes constricting his arms. Leaping to his feet, he snapped the ropes like threads. The gullible muscleman, however, still refused to suspect Delilah, and did not even bother to search the next room, where he would have discovered a posse of heavily-armed Philistines in wait.

Delilah, the original Mata Hari, played her part expertly, sobbing and accusing Samson of lying and offending her. Samson, wanting to toy with her, assured her that he could be seized if she wove together the seven locks of hair in his head and pinned the hairdo under a mesh net. The same scene as before followed. For the third time, Samson was roused with Delilah's screams, "The Philistines are upon you, Samson!" Samson again showed incredible naïveté.

Instead of telling Delilah that he was through, Samson allowed himself to take seriously her threat to leave him. Three or four days later, he finally agreed to tell her how he could be bound. After all, he assured himself, that was a little enough thing if he could continue to enjoy her body.

"I have been a Nazarite to God from my mother's womb," Samson confessed. "If I be shaved, then my strength will leave me, and I shall become weak, and be like any other man" (16:17).

For most of his young life, Samson had been pretending to be tied to God. He had kept the outward form of his Nazarite sect, but actually had been coasting on his parents' faith. Like the person who has evaded all responsibilities of Christian discipleship by explaining, "Oh, but I was baptized a Presbyterian," or, "But I used to go to church every Sunday as a kid back in Kalamazoo," or "My father was a deacon, my mother sang in the choir, and Aunt Bessie taught Sunday school for fifty-five years," Samson thought it was enough to have religious connections. Actually, of course, Samson's Nazarite affiliation had sunk from being empty ritual to silly superstition.

Still not suspecting Delilah's duplicity, Samson spent a passionate evening with her, then heaved into a deep sleep. He groggily opened his eyes when Delilah shrieked that the Philistines were coming. To his horror, he found that his girl friend had shaved him completely bald! Powerless, he was jumped and subdued by a band of Philistines. He struggled frantically, but he could not prevent them from gouging out his eyes.

More than Samson's strength was gone. ". . . he did not know that the Lord had left him" (16:20). Samson had defected from serving God. And God, for Samson, finally ceased to exist.

There seems to be a spiritual law which implies that one may lose a sense of the reality of the Wholly Other through prolonged refusal to obey Him. As the fragile mystic Simone Weil once put it, "If we remain deaf, He comes back again and again like a beggar, but also like a beggar, one day He stops coming."

4

The Outsider

YOUNG WIDOWS are made to feel like used merchandise in the marriage market. Nobody knew this better than Ruth. Therefore, she determinedly turned down the advice that she return home and try to find another husband.

Besides, she still thought of herself as Mahlon's wife. Their marriage had been short, but she had been happy. She had enjoyed their time together and had counted on his support. True to her name (*Ruth* comes from the word meaning *companion* in Hebrew) she had committed her life to pleasing Mahlon. Life had been beautiful.

Suddenly and cataclysmically, it all ended. Mahlon was dead.

Ruth experienced the devastating grief of losing her husband. True, she went through the funeral ceremonies and showed the conventional forms of expressing grief. All the crying and all the praying in the world, however, could not fill the aching emptiness. She longed for the sound of her man's footsteps coming up the path for his evening meal; she yearned for exchanged glances, the secret jokes, the small talk in the darkness, the touch of his hand.

Ruth wished that there had been babies. At least, Mahlon might have lived in some way through his children, and some living reminder of him would remain. Ruth sobbed to herself that her Mahlon was even denied the immortality of having his name

continued through a child. Knowing what a disgrace being childless was in her culture, Ruth groaned, realizing that she was
branded as a failure by her society which placed such a premium
on childbearing. And with all the men in Mahlon's family dead,
including his father and only brother, Ruth knew that no one
would be able to carry on her husband's line. Ruth grieved that
Mahlon's name and family now were extinct. Part of her tears
came from brooding on the fact that she and the man she had
loved had no children.

Perhaps, though, it was just as well. Ruth could guess what a
desperately difficult time a widow with small children had. It was
hard enough being a widow without the added worries of youngsters to feed. In that male-dominated society, women were frequently regarded as chattel. A widow was treated as a nuisance
and a liability.

Ruth wondered what widowhood would mean for her. She
remembered vividly the ancient crones on the fringe of every
female gathering. Ruth recalled the hard lines in their faces
brought on by poverty and loneliness. Would this be her life? Ruth
saw herself doomed to eke out her living by scratching at a small
garden, by accepting a few scraps of handouts, by pawning or
selling her few meager treasures. As a widow, she would lose her
comeliness and wither into another shrivelled-up toothless husband-
less hag, derided by everyone. Her existence would consist of
joining the dreary procession of those in black shawls, shuffling
from a tiny room to the village well each morning. Widows were
surplus articles in the economy, and Ruth sensed immediately that
Mahlon's death had suddenly and drastically reduced her value.
Minor matters such as food and shelter which she had previously
taken for granted loomed as major problems. How would she have
enough to eat? Where would she turn for a place to stay? Ruth
surmised that as a widow she was really not wanted anywhere.

Ruth thought of the requisite in her husband's religion requiring
the next living brother to look after a deceased brother's wife and
family. It was a humane regulation. However, she sighed, it was
useless in her case, because Mahlon's only brother Chilion, was
also dead. She remembered with a heavy feeling, that *all* of the

men in her husband's immediate family were gone, leaving only a
trio of widows: Naomi, her mother-in-law, Orpah, her sister-in-
law, and herself. Who would make the decisions? Who would be
the breadwinner?

Ruth felt terribly alone. She wondered how she would continue
without Mahlon.

Her desolation was accentuated because she was an outsider
everywhere. Originally, Ruth had been a Moabite girl, but she
had turned her back on her own tribe when she married Mahlon,
a young Hebrew settler. She felt the hostility and resentment of
her own people because she had spurned young Moabite men to
marry Mahlon. Ruth sensed that after her marriage, she was an
outsider among her own tribesmen. Although she and Mahlon
continued to live in the territory of Moab, she knew that neither
she nor any of her husband's family were accepted or wanted.

And Ruth was aware that she was an outsider among her husband's people. She quickly learned that Mahlon took immense pride
in being born a Hebrew, part of God's Chosen People, Israel.
Ruth observed the feeling of kinship and loyalty among the
Israelites, and felt some sense of embarrassment because she
could not claim Israelite birth. Although Mahlon's own immediate family, especially his mother Naomi, accepted Ruth
completely and showed her the deepest affection, Ruth picked up
the impression that other Israelites regarded Ruth as something
of a second-class citizen. In fact, Ruth had heard that in Mahlon's
faith, there were even rules forbidding Hebrew boys to marry non-
Hebrew girls. There was, moreover, a long history of bad relationships between the Hebrews and the Moabites. From her earliest
childhood, Ruth had heard of the raids and reprisals back and forth
for generations between Moabites and Hebrews. When she had
thrown in her lot with the Hebrews by marrying Mahlon, Ruth
felt the tensions and enmities from both sides.

What should she do? Her husband's brother's widow, Orpah,
was also a Moabite girl and had returned to her own people after
mourning her husband's death. Ruth considered following her
sister-in-law.

She rejected the idea, however, knowing that she would be a

stranger among her Moabite relatives. Even her own kin would give her little support. She would have to make her own way, and could not count on her people in Moab.

What security could anyone find in life, Ruth wondered? She knew that Mahlon and his family *had* a sense of security, a quality of stability about them. Knowing her husband and his people, especially Naomi, Mahlon's mother, Ruth had long sensed that their strength came from their relationship to their God.

Ruth, however, remembered that she was a Moabite, and therefore an outsider to the community of Mahlon's and Naomi's God. As a non-Israelite, she had no badge of being born a Hebrew, and therefore no claim on her husband's family's God. She wondered whether or not this God would receive her, an outsider.

In fact, Ruth remembered that she did not know very much about this God, except what she had picked up from her husband or Naomi. Ruth realized that she had not been very involved in the worship and could not be considered very religious.

Nonetheless, Ruth decided to commit herself to God. Telling Naomi, her mother-in-law, of her decision, Ruth announced "Your God [shall be] my God" (Ruth 1:16).

Perhaps you have hesitated to commit yourself to the God who has confronted us in love through Jesus Christ. You might have shied away, protesting that you are not part of the *In* group. Or, you demur from committing your life to Him, saying that you cannot dare to claim His strength and comfort because you have not deserved it.

"How can I expect Him to remember me when I've never remembered Him," a salesman protested recently, feeling reluctant to turn to the One whom he'd ignored most of his life.

You may not remember Him. But He remembers you!

In the closing lines of *Doctor Zhivago,* a commissar attempts to supply the details on what eventually happened to Lara: that she apparently died somewhere in a labor camp in the East, a nameless number on a list that got misplaced.

You are never a forgotten statistic to the God who sought you at the Cross and Resurrection. Someday, you will want to respond to that searching concern. You will want to commit yourself to Him as the only One who can strengthen you in your loneliness and insecurity.

Ruth committed herself to the God whom she had never known too well. Although she had no certainty or proof that her husband's and mother-in-law's God would accept her, she threw her entire future on Him.

Ruth immediately learned that God's commitment to her more than matched hers to Him. And she also perceived that His commitment extended to those around her. Ruth responded to God's care to her by caring for others.

She looked around her and the first person she noticed was her mother-in-law, Naomi. Ruth suddenly realized that Naomi was also a widow, and was also an outsider. Here was an elderly woman who also needed companionship and assistance. Ruth *could* have locked herself inside her own problems and loneliness, and thrown away the key. Instead, she empathized with Naomi. "Life can be bitter to the very bone when one is poor, and woman, and alone," Ruth knew long before John Masefield. As one needy, lonely person to another, Ruth extended herself to her own mother-in-law.

As she reached out to those immediately around her, starting with Naomi, Ruth discovered afresh that the more love she gave, the more she received. She was surprised by that ancient paradox that when love is given away in huge, reckless amounts to others, God's care is most real.

On the Cross, Jesus glanced at His Mother and His close friend, John, noticing that each stood stricken and isolated. In one of the tenderest and most meaningful incidents in the Bible, Jesus asked Mary to take in John as a son, and instructed John to look after Mary as his own mother.

God gives lonely, needy people to one another. God's own medicine for the ache of the loneliness of being an outsider is caring for those immediately at hand who are in need. The pain of living as an outsider is eased not by drugs, liquor, prescription, hobbies, or escapes, but by a responsibility for others. Ruth discovered that God gave her to her mother-in-law, and her mother-in-law to her. Ruth also smiled as she learned God meant to have another kind of family relationship. She identified with the community of faith, the people of Israel.

It was not easy. Ruth felt acutely self-conscious. After all, she was (1) a Moabitess, and (2) a widow. Ruth knew that she had no kinship with God's people except the tenuous, indirect ties of an in-law relationship. Penniless and unimportant, she was aware of how little she had to contribute. In spite of her apparent uselessness, however, Ruth insisted on joining with God's people.

"Entreat me not to leave you or to return from following you," Ruth told her mother-in-law, "For where you go, I will go, and where you lodge, I will lodge; your people shall be my people . . ." (Ruth 1:16).

Ruth, the young widow who felt like such an outsider, learned that God's Community does not depend on the usual ties holding people together.

The Church, the "new Israel," "God's people" is such a collection of lonely outsiders today. We stalk each other as anxious strangers. Because we know that we may not be able to make claims on each other through the usual human way of sharing similar interests or finding each other attractive or being kinfolk, we approach each other warily. We feel unimportant. We think we have so little to share with others.

God welds all of us Ruth-like people into new community of trust and concern through Him who moves among us as Risen Lord. Christ, who loves us into being insiders in God's Creation, inducts us into a new family—the Church!

5

The Nobody

ADOLESCENCE is the age of establishing a dominant, positive sense of personhood. *Who Am I?* is the Number One question.

Identity Crisis is the current popular label, but the syndrome is as old as the Bible.

Young Samuel grew up in a time of confusion and despair. Israel's sunny summer of heroics and poetry under Joshua and Deborah had dimmed, followed by a winter of slump and defeat. Joshua and Deborah and the other Judges died. There were no more charismatic chiefs to rally the Israelite clans in emergencies.

In obedience to a vow made before his birth by his parents, the boy Samuel was deposited at the Israelite shrine at Shiloh to be raised by the elderly head priest named Eli. Little Samuel became an apprentice shrine-attendant, or sort of a junior-grade Levite.

The boy was put to work in the Shiloh sanctuary, lighting the seven-branch lampstand each evening and extinguishing it each morning, and doing other jobs under Eli's supervision. He learned the lore of Israel as he worked near the Ark of the Covenant, the gold-covered wooden box which symbolized the residence of the Lord. Each year, he saw his father and mother, Elkanah and Hannah, when they made their annual pilgrimage to Shiloh. Samuel each year received a new sanctuary apron (called an

ephod) which his mother had sewed. He wore it because he was
an understudy for the shrine staff.

Others on the shrine staff—notably Eli's own sons, Hophni and
Phinehas—were hardly models for young Samuel. Hophni and
Phinehas, in fact, disgraced the shrine with their greed and immorality. Their habit of exploiting their office to grab choice of-
ferings and carouse with female worshipers lowered the ethical
and spiritual tone of all Israel. Eli, although personally blameless,
contented himself with a few mild reprimands and pleas for re-
straint instead of tossing his sons out of office. The weak and
indulgent Eli shielded his boys—and was guilty of promoting the
moral deterioration of the Israelites.

Adolescence for young Samuel was a time of confusion. He was
away from home. He had little link with his family. Samuel had a
poor sense of personal history as embodied in his parents. He had
few of the usual opportunities to secure a personal meaning of
adult manhood by associating with his own father.

Samuel pondered the enigma *Who Am I?* Many nights, he lay
awake, trying to peel away the onion layers of his own inner
existence, imagining that he might uncover some basic core of
personhood, might find some *real me.* His search for a psyche,
however, left him lonely and perplexed.

The boy, lacking a sense of personhood, was weak in affirming,
strong in opposing. Adolescent Samuel had endless criticisms of
Eli, the shrine, the country, his parents, his times. Fragmented
and inwardly fragile, young Samuel tended to see himself, however, as a disorganized blur.

Furthermore, Samuel had few other strong adults to emulate.
When he looked to Eli, Samuel encountered an old man (so fat
that he eventually died from toppling from a stool and breaking his
neck) and so ineffective that his own sons' scandals were the talk
of the tribes. An active twelve-year-old boy could hardly find a
sense of personal identity from association with an elderly half-
blind bumbler who had failed with his own sons. Where else
could young Samuel turn? Certainly not to the dissolute roisterers,
Hophni and Phinehas. Samuel's boyhood had loneliness and un-

certainty. The adolescent Samuel had little opportunity to gain a sense of being a distinctive, valued human being from his surroundings.

Unless some sense of personal esteem and dignity grows during adolescence, a person is torn in different directions by inner tensions and outer pulls. "I just can't take hold, Mom, I can't take hold of some kind of life," sighs young Biff in *Death of a Salesman*.

Josephus, the ancient Jewish historian, reports that Samuel was twelve—almost the age of *bar mitzvah* (becoming a *son of the law*) or assuming adult responsibilities—on the night when he was confronted by the Voice.

It started the same as any other night for Samuel in the Shiloh shrine. At sundown, he had lighted the seven-branched lamp, which was kept burning until sunrise in the sanctuary. Young Samuel lay down and slept on a mat nearby. Shortly before dawn ("the lamp of God had not yet gone out . . ." (1 Samuel 3:3),) Samuel was wakened by the Voice.

Samuel, asuming that it was the aged Eli calling, obediently got up and sleepily walked through the sanctuary to where the old man was asleep. Samuel roused Eli, but was perplexed to hear that Eli had not called. Returning to his bed, Samuel dozed off. A second time, Samuel woke up, certain that he had been called by Eli. Again, he hurried to Eli's side, only to be told to go back to sleep.

A third time, Samuel drifted into sleep, and a third time Samuel was wakened. "Samuel . . . Samuel . . ." the Voice repeated. Perplexed, Samuel wandered to where the elderly priest was softly snoring, and disturbed Eli's slumber by speaking, ". . . Here I am, for you called me . . ." (3:8).

Samuel previously had experienced a vague, poorly-defined sense of God, known only a second-hand religion. ". . . Samuel did not know the Lord," reports the Biblical writer, "and the word of the Lord had not yet been revealed to him" (1 Samuel 3:7). Samuel not only had few meaningful insights into himself, but little personal, existential understanding of God.

Samuel did not yet comprehend that God has no set schedule,

that God springs His own surprises. God, Samuel could not understand, decides to introduce Himself sometimes when least expected.

God has no formal office hours, no specified working period. God delights in intruding at awkward moments, such as when we think we are alone and unobserved. He even surprises us by making Himself real in places we think unlikely—sometimes even as at church on Sunday at 11 A.M.! The Presence whispers to our consciousnesses when He pleases.

Samuel was not dazzled by a sensational disclosure by the Presence. In fact, young Samuel mistook his being awakened for a call from Eli. There were no dramatic touches. There were no pulse-quickening visions of heaven, no booming bass voices from the echo chamber rousing everyone in Shiloh. Instead, there was a persistent, repeated summons to Samuel.

Don't try to literalize Samuel's call by God. It is pointless to argue whether or not the Voice could have been picked up on a tape recorder. We smudge the fragile beauty of the description of Samuel's experience when we try to externalize the internal. Anytime we attempt to express objectively what is essentially something subjective, we end up making it sound slightly silly and awkward.

"Samuel . . . Samuel . . . Samuel . . ." Samuel had to have his call repeated several times. God must sometimes knock repeatedly on a person's consciousness.

And Samuel had to have his call interpreted by another person. Bewildered, Samuel did not grasp the meaning of the Presence's persistence until Eli told him, ". . . Go, lie down; and if he calls you, you shall say, 'Speak, Lord, for thy servant hears . . .'" (3:9).

Even though we each receive what Calvin called the *private call,* it is always a public matter. We need each other as God's community to interpret the confusing signals we think we hear. Although there we each acknowledge our own personal summons by the Living One, it is never purely private or individualistic. Anytime we try to be loners in religion, we end up as losers, for God wills community. We Samuels always need an Eli. We depend on each other in the Church for aid and support in deciphering what God sometimes beams to us in our solitude.

"Samuel!" Unmistakably, the summons came again. Samuel knew that the Lord had words for him. The boy timidly responded, ". . . Speak, for thy servant hears" (3:10).

Young Samuel acknowledged that the Lord called his name *Samuel*. Before the Presence, Samuel was awakened to his real identity. Samuel (Samuel means *name of the Lord*) was introduced to the real Samuel when the Voice called him by name.

Samuel until the time of God's call had been a confused nobody. Before God, Samuel learned that he was somebody. Transformed from being a boyish bundle of bewilderment, Samuel found coherence in his life through his commitment to the Lord. The boy who previously was a groping nonentity was given a clear and unified sense of identity by God. Samuel knew that he belonged to the Lord! Therefore, he knew who he was, where he stood, where he came from, and where he was going! With God, Samuel had an implicit set of goals and standards. And with such goals and standards, Samuel had a sense of self to stand on. Although his society was degenerating, his nation was humiliated, his clergymen were corrupt, his people were demoralized, Samuel was prevented from declining into a brooding neurotic. Samuel knew that God had conferred a new personality on him.

Once, on the Pennsylvania frontier toward the close of the eighteenth century, a settler's child was abducted by marauding Indians. The distraught father searched tirelessly for the boy. Years passed. No word was received about the youngster. Traders and scouts told the father that it was useless to try to track down his son. At immense personal risk, the father began the practice of visiting Indian villages, where he asked permission to whisper just one word to the boys of the tribe who would be the same age of his son. The father, invariably dismissed by this time as a harmless crackpot, would be seen approaching each young brave, and whispering, *"Tommy!"* in the lad's ear.

Finally, after incredible hardships, one day the father entered an Indian village across the mighty Ohio, patiently went through the by-then familiar process of whispering his son's name in the ears of the boys who would have been as old as his own boy. *"Tommy!"* he insistently muttered. Suddenly, one boy turned. Some almost-forgotten memory had been evoked, some dimly-remembered chord had been struck. The boy's eyes blinked. He paused, then struggled to articulate the reply, "Father!"

Our real identities come when we are found and called by the seeking Father. He knows us by name, not as part of a huge, impersonal, dehumanized, bureaucratic mass. We are given significance in our own eyes only as we become aware that we are given the standing of sons and daughters by The One. We are saved from existing alone and without a future. We are rescued from being preoccupied with a lost past. This is the meaning of the Gospel! This is the message of Him who sought us through the crucified, Risen Lord!

We will be diffused nobodies until, before Christ, we learn that we are beloved somebodies. Our identity is bestowed only by Him. A sense of personhood is a gift, and is given as we are aware that we are recognized by name by the One who came to seek and save us who were lost.

And so immediately after God called Samuel by his name, Samuel replied, ". . . Speak, for thy servant hears" (3:10). When Samuel heard what the Lord had to say, however, he wished that he had not asked. Samuel gasped as a horrible message of doom for Eli and his family was spelled out. God was bringing a day of reckoning for the top religious leaders of the nation, starting with Eli, Samuel learned.

The words from the Lord seared the boy's ears. "On that day, I will fulfill against Eli all that I have spoken concerning his house, from beginning to end. And I tell him that I am about to punish his house for ever, for the iniquity which he knew, because his sons were blaspheming God, and he did not restrain them" (3:12–13).

Samuel shook with fright. The sentence on Eli seemed so total, so severe. Samuel could not close his eyes or sleep, thinking of the horrors in store for Eli. In his mind, Samuel could picture the defeat and indignities as the Philistines swept through the country, the destruction of the lovely old shrine at Shiloh, the deaths of

Eli's sons and the end of Eli's family. Samuel knew what a crushing blow the loss of the sons would be to Eli, for the worse possible dishonor for an Israelite was to die without a surviving son.

Tears came as Samuel recalled that he had been also told that old Eli would perish in the coming halocaust. Samuel felt an affection toward the elderly priest. Although Samuel had often been disgusted by Eli's ineffectiveness, he remembered that the fat old man had tried in his bumbling way to act as a spiritual coach.

The hardest part of all, however, was the task laid on Samuel. Samuel understood that God intended him to deliver the message pronouncing Eli's sentence. The last thing in the world Samuel wanted was to offend the old priest who had befriended him. Samuel sobbed to himself. Why was the Lord laying such a burden on him? Samuel asked. Why could the call of God not have been a pleasant, private message of reassurance? Samuel could not sleep that entire night, agonizing over the meaning of God's call.

God's call is an invitation to the icy plunge of service, never permission to be tucked under an electric blanket of personal comfort. The Voice, Samuel discovered, did not glorify Samuel; rather God summoned Samuel to do what Samuel did not want to do: to denounce the evil of Eli's family.

One test of the reality of God in one's life is whether or not His Presence means some stomach-tightening tensions and brow-wrinkling decisions as well as confidence and stability. God's call most likely is to some unpleasant tasks. It is never a coronation, always a cross.

Samuel anguished throughout the remainder of that night. At the first hint of dawn, he rose and started his chores. He hoped that Eli would have forgotten the times Samuel awakened him. Above all, Samuel hoped that the priest would not ask any questions. The shaken and frightened boy did not want to discuss the night's events, particularly the disclosure by the Presence. When he heard Eli beginning to stir, young Samuel tried to avoid the old man.

Wheezing, Eli waddled over to where Samuel pretended to be busy. "What was it that he told you?" (3:17). Eli cautiously asked. Cagey old Eli was careful in his wording; he wasn't certain that

Samuel's voice was the Lord's. There are many voices in the night when one is a youngster and alone, Eli knew.

Eli knew that voices and messages from God must be tested. The priest was correctly wary of accepting reports of divine commands. Only when he heard Samuel's message was Eli ready to grant its authenticity. Eli was wise enough to know that God's call brings a sword. With tears, Eli acknowledged the validity of Samuel's experience of the Presence. "It is the Lord," Eli whispered when he heard the message of death, disgrace and destruction.

Samuel stood quietly. He pitied the old man. For a few minutes, neither spoke. Samuel contemplated the unrest, the changes, the problems which lay ahead. There would be near-constant personal and national turmoil, he was certain. Many, including his mentor and friend, Eli, would not survive.

Samuel fleetingly remembered how only a few hours earlier, he had quivered with fear and uncertainty. It seemed like a lifetime ago, in a sense. He had been a different Samuel, a little nobody. Samuel smiled to himself. He knew that God had bestowed a sense of personhood on him. And he was confident that God had given him the inner stamina to stand up to anything.

As God's man, Samuel gently led Eli to a seat.

6
The Loser

THE LAST THING in the world the hulking young giant was looking for that afternoon was a call to be king. Lost donkeys, not leadership, were his main thoughts. With enormous strides which left his servant panting to keep up, the huge youngster had roamed the rocky hills for three days, trying to locate the strayed livestock for his father. When the servant suggested consulting Samuel for advice, the rancher's big son agreed.

Unconscious of his commanding presence (". . . There was not a man among the people of Israel more handsome than he; from his shoulders upward, he was taller than any of the people of Israel" (1 Samuel 9:2). Saul, the strapping boy, strode purposefully up to the aged prophet, Samuel. "Give me some clues where I may find my lost donkeys," Saul bluntly began. He was disconcerted, however, when the old prophet looked up with a strange expression and replied reverently that Saul was to be the guest of honor at a feast.

Saul, remembering the donkeys, started to protest. He felt slightly reassured when the old man told him that the donkeys had been located, but Saul was puzzled by the invitation to the feast. What did it mean? Saul wondered. Why should he, a complete stranger, a shepherd kid from the hinterland be invited? It mystified Saul.

Saul demurred. He noticed that the elderly prophet became insistent. Saul protested that he was a nobody, a member of the smallest tribe, the Benjaminites, and an insignificant member of a little-known clan within the Benjaminites, and did not deserve any honors.

The more Saul humbly tried to decline, however, the more delighted Samuel became. Completely puzzled, Saul reluctantly consented to go to the feast. He was further perplexed when the prophet led him to the most prominent seat and handed him the choicest pieces of meat. Saul sat politely, but wondered why he was getting all the attention.

The following day, the towering young herdsman was led aside by Samuel. When Saul and Samuel were alone, and Saul was wondering what was going to happen next, he was ordered to kneel. Awkwardly, the boy sank to his knees. He hardly noticed that by kneeling, his head was at the same height as Samuel's.

Saul suddenly saw what Samuel intended to do. He noticed that old Samuel had a vial of the special oil used only for anointing princes and he understood that Samuel meant to anoint him! Saul started to cry out. He did not want to be anointed anything. Seeing the firm look on Samuel's face, however, Saul realized that he could not argue.

Saul bowed his head respectfully as Samuel told him quietly, ". . . you shall reign over the people of the Lord and you will save them from the hand of their enemies round about . . ." (10:1). Saul became aware that he had been consecrated as one having divine inspiration.

At the same time, he felt unsure of himself and afraid. He asked himself how he could be certain of this call. Furthermore, he was anxious about what his father was thinking about his long absence and the lost donkeys.

Saul sighed with relief when Samuel assured him that the donkeys were safe and his father was not worried. As for the startling secret known only to Saul and Samuel, Saul heard with some surprise that he would discover for himself that he truly had been anointed by God. He listened dubiously as the old seer predicted that, on his way home the big ranch boy would fall in with a group of prophets.

"Then the spirit of the Lord will come mightily upon you," Samuel assured Saul, "and you shall prophesy with them and be turned into another man" (10:6). Then, seven days later, Samuel stated, a public investiture would be held for Saul at Gilgal.

By the time the towering young Benjaminite left Samuel, however, he was no longer bewildered. In the words of 1 Samuel 10:9, ". . . God gave him another heart."

Anytime God calls a person to an apparently impossible task, He gives that person a new heart. Before anyone can *do* anything, he first must *be* someone. *Being* comes before *doing*.

John Wesley, grimly trying to serve Christ as a joyless prig in Georgia, returned to England discouraged and ineffective, crying, "I went to America to convert the Indians, but oh! who shall convert me?" He had tried to *do* before he had learned to *be*. Not until the meeting in Aldersgate Street in London did he experience, "the change which God works in the heart through faith in Christ, I felt my heart strangly moved." From that hour when God gave him a new heart, Wesley became the man who brought Christianity back to England, if not the English-speaking world. He launched the great evangelical revival of the eighteenth century which stamped British and American personal character, social ideals, morals, education, and worship practices.

Saul, given a new heart, no longer had the heart of a rough, insensitive ranch hand. After his private call through Samuel, Saul knew that he carried the heart of a general, a statesman, a king. He joined ecstatically, as Samuel had predicted, in the singing and prophesying of a troop of joyous worshipers. And when he returned home and an uncle cross-examined him about his encounter with Samuel, Saul obediently said nothing about the anointing. His new heart meant humility. He eagerly waited for Samuel to make public the momentous announcement about his kingship.

A week later, Samuel gathered the tribes at Mizpah. There was an air of jubilant expectation. Samuel had promised to announce the name of the man who would be Israel's first king, the prince who would pull the loosely-organized tribes together after the stinging humiliation of Philistine domination.

The method of choosing the king was the time-honored practice of casting lots. First, lots were cast to single out one tribe from the twelve. The tribe of Benjamin was chosen as the one from which the king would come. Next lots were drawn among the Benjaminites to select one clan. Still more lots narrowed the clans down to one clan, and then one family within the clan, until Kish's family was picked as the one from whom the ruler would be chosen. Eventually, everyone was eliminated except young Saul.

Saul had stood shyly at the edge of the crowd watching the proceedings. As each toss of the lots increased the likelihood that he would be selected, however, Saul grew more uncertain of himself and fearful of the future. He peered over the crowd, his great height giving him an obstructed view of the entire gathering. How, he asked himself, could he ever dare to assume the leadership of all these people? Perspiring nervously, Saul heard with great misgivings the announcement that the last roll of the lots reduced the list to Kish's family. Kish! That was the name of his father. Saul felt panicky.

Suddenly Saul bolted and ran behind the piles of baggage, tents, feed baskets and equipment piled to one side of the gathering. Crouching between two large bundles, the young man tried to burrow into the middle of the heap of luggage and hide.

A moment later, he shuddered as he heard his name shouted. *"Saul!"* Saul cowered, trying to make his huge frame more compact. It was, of course, impossible. He felt hands eagerly tugging at his shoulders.

As he walked forward, propelled by hundreds of cheering Israelites, Saul blinked. He heard the aged prophet shouting above the din, "Do you see him whom the Lord has chosen? There is none like him among all the people . . ." (10:24). In spite of feeling dazed by the acclaim, Saul felt a tremor of excitement. Saul realized that his private anointing was publicly ratified. Old Samuel's words, Saul suddenly thought, had been confirmed. Saul told himself that God meant him to be Israel's king.

After Mizpah, everyone went home and everything lapsed into the familiar quiet pattern. The towering boy-king returned to the family ranch. He knew that in spite of the hoopla and cheers at Mizaph he still had not proved himself among the people. When some of his countrymen snickered and made contemptuous comments such as " 'How can this man save us?' " (10:27) Saul wisely kept quiet.

Saul's real initiation as king soon came. While plowing one day, he was brought word that the Ammonites, a tribe of desert warriors who swept across the Jordan on periodic raids, were preying on hapless Israelite tribesmen along the eastern border and were preparing to attack Jabesh-gilead. Saul acted decisively. Slaughtering his oxen, he hacked the carcasses into pieces. Just as the fiery cross carried though the Scottish Highlands rallied the clans, the bloodly chunks of Saul's oxen summoned the tribes of Israel to war, with the grim warning that anyone holding back would be butchered like the oxen. The Tribes responded immediately. Saul led the young nation to its first victory. Jabesh-gilead never forgot its debt to Saul; years later, when nearly everyone else had defected, Saul could always count on the loyalty of the men from Jabesh.

In the intoxication of beating back the Ammonites, some superpatriots wanted to execute those who has scoffed at Saul after his presentation as king at Mizpah. Knowing that he was secure as the unchallenged ruler, Saul magnanimously refused. No longer the blushing princeling, Saul the tested leader did not hide or object when Samuel called Israel to gather for an impressive coronation ceremony.

After a farewell address by Samuel, the monarchy was formally established. ". . . They made Saul king before the Lord in Gilgal . . ." the author of 1 Samuel 11:15 states. Note well the words, *before the Lord;* it was understood that Saul, although king, was still very much the subject of the Lord. England's Henry V directed the 115th Psalm be sung after the victory at Agincourt, prostrating himself on the ground and ordering his soldiers to do the same when the words were sounded, "Not unto us, O Lord, not unto us, but unto thy name give glory." In the same way Israel's Saul knew well that his victory and his throne were *before the Lord*. It was young Saul's finest hour. The orbit of his career reached its apogee at Gilgal.

Some years after World War I, the French writer Emile Verhaeren described how he had allowed the brutality and hate of the war to murder the ideals and dreams he had carried as a young man before 1914. Verhaeren dedicated his book, TO THE MAN I USED TO BE. Many years after Gilgal, after a career of insane jealousy and cruelty, Saul remembered the man he used to be. The memory, however, was too much. Unable by that time to be the young Saul before God he once had been, old Saul took his own life.

What happened? How could such a career of such brilliant promise end so tragically?

The young king was commanded by wise old Samuel to throw off the Philistine yoke. With their secret weapon of iron, the Philistines had become powerful overlords. Saul's forces threw down the gauntlet by capturing the Philistine outpost at Geba. Making the nearby village of Gibeah his headquarters, Saul dislodged the Philistines from part of the hill country and roused other Israelite tribesmen to gather behind him. The Philistines, determined to save face and avenge this insult, mustered their forces. Saul, however, was warned by Samuel not to attack until he had received God's blessing. And he would receive that blessing, he was told, when Samuel appeared in a week's time. Meanwhile, he and his untested troops were told to sit tight.

As the well-equipped, well-trained Philistine troops began to gather at Michmash, Saul's raw recruits grew restless. Each day additional numbers of battle-hardened Philistines rolled into Michmash. Saul's men began to show symptoms of panic. Saul suspected that the longer he delayed, the lesser the odds were for victory. Attack while he still had the advantage, he told himself. His green battalions, actually nothing more than a collection of shepherds, farmers and shopkeepers armed with makeshift weapons, would be no match against Philistine chariots and cavalry. Each day that he waited, Saul noted that there were reports of increasing numbers of desertions from his frightened army.

We may raise our eyebrows about the Biblical reference to the Israelite forces being dependent upon God's blessing. It sounds arrogant to us to hear the implication that God would bless the Israelites' campaign to slaughter the Philistines. The point of the Biblical narrative is not that the Lord was on the Israelite side but that Saul was meant to be obedient to God. Saul was merely a trustee of the authority given to him. Although king, he had limited powers. God alone had final and supreme rule. Saul, given a *new heart* by God and installed as king *before the Lord* had been plainly informed that all his powers were derivative, not residual.

When Samuel had still not come at the appointed time, Saul had had enough waiting. He took matters into his own hands. Impulsively, he went through the motions of worship. Young King Saul, anxious to get the formalities of the sacrifice to God out of the way so that he could attack, offered the sacrifice himself—an act reserved for a priest. In effect, Saul put himself above God's law.

When Samuel arrived shortly after Saul had made his perfunctory act of worship, Saul lamely made excuses. The elderly prophet, quivering with indignation over Saul's disobedience to God, sputtered, "You have done foolishly; you have not kept the commandment of the Lord your God . . . but now your kingdom shall not continue" (13:13–14).

Israel, Samuel knew, needed a king, not a self-appointed priest. Saul, who presumed he could take over priestly functions, had become the kind of man who could also presume to take over for God. Furthermore, Samuel noted that Saul had reduced worship to magic. God, for Saul, had become a lucky piece. Sacrifice was merely a gimmick to get God to bless the battle. To Samuel's dismay, his young protege had become power-hungry and had overreached himself. Such insubordination, before God, Samuel knew, would ultimately bring ruin to Saul.

The medieval city-state of Venice, rarely allowing faith to interfere with fortune-making, had the motto, *Siamo Veneziani, poi Cristiani:* "We are Venetians; after that we are Christians." Saul, obeying his own impulses and disregarding God, held the same mistaken priorities.

When we are Venetians or anything else ahead of being God's

person, we're in trouble. We are forced to live a lie. The pretense of trying to convince ourselves that it is necessary for God's will to be secondary and our own will primary means existing with an increasingly-elaborate web of illusions. And when we live only with illusions, we gradually become paranoid.

The disobedient Saul became a near-classic case study of an emotionally disturbed man. At first, the erosion of his character was almost imperceptible. Later, however, Saul deteriorated into an extreme manic-depressive, alternating between sudden, unpredictable violent outbursts, hurling his spear at anyone who crossed him, and prolonged bouts of deep morbid brooding.

In spite of Saul's disobedience before the battle of Michmash, Samuel did not give up on Saul. Samuel, however, noted privately that the young monarch began to show disturbing signs of lacking the vision and imagination to press a successful campaign against the Philistines. Uncertain and hesitant, Saul paced and issued unnecessary orders while his youthful son, Jonathan, daringly reconnoitering the Philistine fortified positions, learned how jumpy the Philistine forces were and led a quick attack which caused the Philistines to panic. Saul, however, threw away opportunities for total victory by silly commands such as prohibiting his men to eat until after dark and passing the death sentence on his son Jonathan for unwittingly defying orders.

The final turning-point in Saul's personality deterioration took place during the Amalekite campaign. Like the Ammonites, whom Saul had whipped early in his career, the Amalekites preyed on settlements along Israel's eastern frontier. Samuel was shrewdly aware that Israel could not fight a two-front war, and that the country would not be safe as long as the Amalekites marauded on one border and the Philistine forts stood on the other. In the name of the Lord, the old prophet commanded Saul to take advantage of the lull in the continual skirmishing against the Philistines and raid the surly Amalekites. Samuel specifically ordered Saul to strike so decisively that the Amalekites would be prevented from molesting Israel in the future. Even Amalekite livestock was to be wiped out.

Saul, however, thought that the rules were made for everyone else but him. Although told to make total war against the Amalekites, Saul, after seizing the initiative, equivocated. He stepped back from carrying out the operation to its conclusion, allowing the Amalekite chieftains to escape to fight another day. The Amalekites, who had harrassed the Israelites for generations, would continue to be a threat.

Saul, desirous of boosting his ego, planned to play the mighty hero by marching the Amalekite leaders through streets. Furthermore, instead of destroying the Amalekite livestock, Saul had held on to the best of it for himself. The crowning touch was a fancy monument which Saul ordered put up in his own honor. Like the elegant Hollywood dandy Adolphe Menjou carrying the silver cigarette case inscribed TO ADOLPHE MENJOU, FROM HIS WARMEST ADMIRER, ADOLPHE MENJOU, Saul's monument was the symbol of conceit.

Samuel was incensed. Storming up to Saul, the prophet confronted the king with his insubordination toward God.

Saul indignantly denied any disobedience. ". . . I have performed the commandment of the Lord" (1 Samuel 15:13), he protested. With the self-righteous aplomb of a General Douglas Haig (who before the ill-conceived battle of the Somme in 1916 in which 250,000 British died, confidently wrote, "I feel that every step in my plan has been taken with divine help"), Saul strutted and blared his piety. The sheep and oxen which Samuel heard bleating, Saul smoothly purred, were ". . . to sacrifice to the Lord your God . . ." (1 Samuel 15:15).

Samuel exploded. ". . . the Lord sent you on a mission. . . . Why then did you not obey the voice of the Lord?" (15:18–19).

Obedience to God takes place on specific missions, in the everyday round of acts, commitments and decisions. Obedience to God is never generalized. It must be actualized in specific ways at specific times at specific places. Otherwise, it is nonexistent. "It's not so much that you *can* do it," Jack Dempsey once said about boxing, "but that you *do* it on Saturday night at 10 o'clock at Madison Square Garden," and the same idea holds true with regard to obeying God. Unless obedience to God has a "Saturday-night-at-ten-in-Madison-Square-Garden" concreteness, it is empty.

Young King Saul thought it was enough to be obedient-in-general. When pressed by Samuel, he lamely insisted, "I have obeyed. . . . But the people took the spoil . . . to sacrifice to the Lord . . ." (15:20–21). His air-conditioned conscience allowed him to shift the blame to the people. His "I-have-obeyed-but" attitude betrayed his spirtual decay. Saul had sunk to being a man who, in the words Teddy Roosevelt once used to describe William Howard Taft, "means well feebly."

Samuel dressed down the youthful ruler for his lack of responsibility as leader of the nation. ". . . to obey is better than sacrifice. . . . Because you have rejected the word of the Lord, he has also rejected you from being king" (15:22–23), Samuel coldly announced.

Saul, however, was determined to live by illusions. He refused to confront the falsity in himself. In his illusions, he saw absolute virtues in himself and absolute depravity in others. Having swapped places with God, Saul fancied himself a self-made man, and worshiped his creator. All the dismaying symptoms of moral and psychological schizophrenia began to appear.

The man with illusions about himself, Jesus warned, is in graver danger than almost anyone else. The falsity of claiming to be one thing but in actuality being another is potentially lethal. Small wonder that Jesus' harshest words were directed against the hypocrites. He showed more severity toward the man whose disobedience led him to illusory pretense than toward thieves, adulterers, or even murderers.

Emotionally disturbed? Mentally ill? Call it what you will, but the phrase, "Now the Spirit of the Lord departed from Saul and an evil spirit . . . tormented him" (16:14) sums it up.

Author-Traveler John Gunther used to say that whenever he visited a country and talked to the leading political personalities, he tried to focus on two questions: *What are the real sources of power behind the man? What does he believe in most?* Had Gunther interviewed King Saul about 1000 B.C. at the time of Saul's coronation, he would have learned that the both questions would have been answered by: *The Living God.* If Gunther had returned a few years later, he would have discovered that for Saul, the real source of power and what he believed in most were simply his spear. Inspiration had given way to superstition. The young king, anointed to be the winner, degenerated to being a loser.

7

The Winner

ALTHOUGH the boy knew that he had been secretly selected by the aged prophet-statesman, to be the king to follow Saul, young David wondered. Who would ever acknowledge a beardless, ruddy-faced shepherd?

Even his seven brothers laughed at him as the runt. The youngest and smallest, David was relegated to looking after the sheep. Disgusted at not doing something more exciting, young David spent long hours on the lonely hillsides. He sometimes entertained himself by making up verses to recite as he strummed his lyre. Other times, he picked up tennis ball-sized rocks, placed one on a woven sling, whirled the sling rapidly above his head, and, releasing the one end, fired the stone at an imaginary enemy Philistine. Many times, he used his sling to scare away marauding animals. Most of the time, however, David wished that he could prove himself a man. He gazed pensively at the stars at night, lying on his back in the stone sheep enclosure, pondering how God would ever want him to be the man of destiny for the tribes. It often seemed to young David that his opportunity would never come, but that he would spend his entire life as a solitary shepherd boy.

When three of his older brothers enlisted in King Saul's forces to fight the Philistines, David envied them. He gazed admiringly at his strapping brothers as they polished their weapons and discussed the coming campaign. David longed to march off with them, but knew that they would scorn him as too young, as they had so many times in the past. Resigned to missing the excitement, he dejectedly picked up his lyre and sling, and returned to the flock.

One day, his father asked him to carry some food supplies to his brothers in Saul's army. David, delighted to get away from the sheep and to see where the action was, eagerly set out.

When he approached the encampment, he stopped, wide-eyed with wonder and excitement. David had never seen such a sight. Before him stretched Saul's lines of men, each man heavily armed and ready for battle. Some distance away, drawn up in a line parallel to Saul's forces, stood the Philistine army. Tents, stacks of equipment, piles of baggage, cooking fires, livestock, and bustling messengers filled an enormous area behind each army.

David's breath caught as he watched the biggest man he had ever seen in his life step out of the Philistine ranks and swagger slowly into no-man's land. A hush fell. Nobody moved. David slipped unnoticed through the files of Saul's soldiers and found his brothers.

David did not notice how tense everyone was. Expecting to be welcomed and thanked, he smilingly started to hand the brothers the supplies. He flinched when his oldest brother asked harshly, "Why have you come down? And with whom have you left those few sheep in the wilderness? I know your presumption, and the evil of your heart; for you have come down to see the battle" (1 Samuel 17:28). Wounded at being called down so roughly in public by a big brother, David the kid brother protested, "What have I done now?" (17:29).

David smarted as he remembered how often his brothers had picked on him. He moved down the line of silent, grim-faced troops. Peering between the men, David suddenly noticed that the huge Philistine soldier was still advancing.

The Philistine giant stopped midway between the two armies. With a voice like a roaring bull, the towering enemy trooper insolently challenged any soldier from Saul's army to man-to-man combat. He strutted back and forth, waiting for someone to take up his dare.

David looked around to see who would step up and face the taunting bully. Astonished that no one in Saul's army moved, David asked in boyish innocence why someone didn't accept the challenge. David noticed that his questions made the men near him uncomfortable. As the huge Philistine champion continued to insult Saul's soldiers, David persisted in asking why someone didn't stand up to the giant.

King Saul, overhearing David, called the rugged young shepherd boy to his side. He was surprised and amused when the rugged shepherd boy unceremoniously told him, "Let no man's heart fail because of him [Goliath]; [I] will go and fight with this Philistine" (17:32). Saul smiled and prepared to dismiss young David, telling him, ". . . you are but a youth . . ." (17:33).

Breathlessly, youthful David recounted his exploits against wild animals which had tried to snatch his sheep, and announced he'd made short work of Goliath. Before Saul could interrupt, David proclaimed, "The Lord who delivered me from the paw of the lion . . . and bear will deliver me from the hand of this Philistine . . ." (17:37).

Such grit and guts appealed to Saul. With a hearty laugh and a clap of his big hand, the king told David to have a try, and ordered his men to fit the youngster out in Saul's own armor.

It was hilariously funny to see the boy David trying to maneuver in the heavy plates and clumsy chains, the big helmet and outsized sword of the huge king. Saul and his aides roared with laughter watching David's attempts to move under the mountain of clanking bronze.

David struggled out of Saul's armor and strode determinedly to a nearby brook, where he picked up five rocks. Taking his sling, David boldly walked toward the Philistine champion. He ignored the curses and contempt of the giant, and called, ". . . You come to me with a sword, spear and . . . javelin, but I come to you in the name of the Lord . . . whom you have defied. This day, the Lord will deliver you into my hand, and I will strike you down . . . that all the earth may know that there is God in Israel . . . and that all . . . may know that the Lord saves not with sword and spear . . ." (17:45–47).

Twirling the lethal sling above his head, David suddenly fired a stone with deadly accuracy and force, striking the startled Philistine on the temple. The disabled giant collapsed in a dusty, groaning heap. Swiftly, David rushed to the downed champion, seized the big sword and hacked at the Philistine's neck until he had severed the head.

The shepherd boy suddenly found himself the national hero!

Astonishingly, the cheers and adulation did not go to the lad's head. From the time of his anointing by Samuel, young David had been conscious of the Lord's presence. He carried an unshakable certainty that his career was inextricably involved with God's plans. Such a man, like Oliver Cromwell or John Brown or "Chinese" Gordon burned with the white flame of near-fanaticism for his faith, and proved to be a formidable soldier. When a man announces, ". . . the battle is the Lord's and he will give you into our hand" (17:47), as David did, he has been stiffened not with the starch of oratory but with the steel of prayer.

David, as Saul described him, was merely a stripling, a youth, a young man (17:55–58) when he entered King Saul's service. His winsome mannerisms and pleasant equanimity made him a favorite with Saul and with Jonathan, Saul's son and heir to the throne.

David and Jonathan, the prince, quickly established a brotherly bond, cemented with a covenant or pact which, in effect, bound them together even closer than blood brothers.

Saul came to depend on the young David, leaning on David's spiritual strength and drawing from David's vitality. Insecure because his life was not rooted in God, the deteriorating monarch could find security only by having David nearby.

David noticed that the king showed dismaying symptoms of instability. Taking out his lyre, David softly played chords and quietly sang shepherd songs. The music provided therapy for the distraught Saul. As Saul's moods grew more ugly and his spells grew more frequent, David often found himself playing and singing to soothe the king. Soon, David seemed to be the only person whom

Saul would trust. David was promoted to the royal armor-bearer, or personal attendant and private confidant to Saul.

David's promotion to royal armor-bearer meant that he had to take part in the skirmishes against the Philistines. The poised young musician quickly showed that he also had skills as a soldier. Thrown repeatedly into sorties against the Philistines, David distinguished himself for bravery so often that he became better known as a fighter than as a composer-performer.

David's exploits against the Philistines quickly made his name a household word everywhere. Saul, insecure and suspicious, began to grumble that his young armor-bearer was getting more headlines than the king. One day when the royal entourage returned from an encounter against the Philistines in which David had again covered himself with glory, the women came out of the villages, dancing and shaking tamborines, singing and shouting, "Saul has slain his thousands and David his ten thousands!" Insanely jealous of David, Saul lost the last semblances of self-discipline and emotional stability. The next day, Saul flew into a rage and twice hurled his spear at David trying to pin him to the wall and murder him. David nimbly dodged each time, further infuriating Saul.

Removing David became a fixation with Saul. He commissioned David as commander of his shock troops, assuming that David would be picked off in battle. Instead, he discovered that David rose to greater heights of valor and popularity than before.

His thinking becoming more and more deranged, Saul promised his oldest daughter in marriage if David undertook a particularly risky mission against the Philistines. Saul, figuring that David would end up on the casualty list, was further enraged when David returned a bigger hero than ever. Saul backed down on the marriage deal. When his second daughter, Michal, and David took an interest in each other, Saul deviously contrived another plot to have David killed. As dowry, Saul demanded one hundred dead Philistines, certain that David would never live to return from this raid. The fantastic young warrior came back victorious from this impossible assignment. Sullen and resentful of David's mounting successes, Saul granted him Michal—but concocted new ways to eliminate David as a rival.

An enraged madman, Saul finally put away all pretenses and *ordered* Jonathan and some servants to kill David. Jonathan, however, thwarted this assassination attempt by interceding for his friend David. When David returned to Saul and cordially agreed to play the lyre, Saul suddenly lunged at the young musician. David, with catlike reflexes, ducked in time, but Saul's spear was imbedded in the wall.

David raced out of the palace to his own house. His wife Michal, knowing her father's cunning, insisted that David flee that night through a window. Exactly as Michal guessed, a band of assassins burst into the house shortly after David left.

David felt shaken. There had been too many close brushes with death. He sensed the unreasoning, manic impulses to murder in Saul. David did not want to die. Although he remembered his destiny as God's man, he needed reassurance.

Stealthily, David made his way to old Samuel's place and asked the prophet for help. David soon discovered that he was not safe even at Samuel's. Three different groups came to arrest him, but remained to worship and prophesy with Samuel instead of seizing David. David surmised that it would not be long before Saul himself would lead a party of hired killers to his refuge.

David, however, refused to strike back at the King. In spite of his immense popularity, David made no moves to organize a revolt to displace Saul. David continued to maintain a sense of loyalty toward Saul. He recognized that Saul's creative characteristics were being crushed by dark, terrible emotions, and hoped that Saul would recover his sanity.

At the same time, David was wracked with personal misgivings. He asked himself if he had said or done anything which had helped trigger Saul's emotional tirades. David had a healthy sense of self-doubt. With exceptional maturity, he accepted his share, if any, of blame and responsibility for Saul's problems.

David sought out his trusted ally, Jonathan, asking humbly, ". . . What is my sin before your father that he seeks my life?" (20:1). As God's man, David was willing to admit his faults and seek reconciliation. He asked Jonathan to find if it was safe to return to Saul's court.

David learned shortly that he had to flee for his life. Even Jonathan, David discovered, had nearly been impaled by a spear during Saul's latest violent outburst. Running for his life, David made his way to the wilderness.

The wilderness stretches bleakly and desolately. Nearly uninhabitable, it is an area of enervating heat, steep canyons, rocky wastelands. Wandering in this tortuous land quickly cures a man of ambition.

David wondered why God had selected him to serve as eventual ruler of Israel. He remembered that Samuel had anointed him as God's chosen one, but asked himself why God allowed him to live as a hunted outlaw in the wilderness. Hiding in caves, dodging Saul's relentless patrols and living by his wits sometimes among the surly Philistines, David seemed carried further each day from his destiny as the anointed king-to-be.

There are apparently-endless stretches of wilderness in every person's career. Life in the wilderness, to the man without a living faith, seems to support the old Russian myth that God has an idiot brother whom He sometimes leaves to tend the shop. David's wilderness tested his faith and tempered his soul.

On the run, David received a sword and food from the priest at the village of Nob. He was heartsick to hear soon after, however, that Saul massacred the entire village in reprisal for the priest's aid. Fleeing to the Philistines, the young fugitive tried to enlist as an anonymous soldier under the king of Gath. He was recognized, however, and escaped only by feigning insanity.

David escaped to a large cave near Adullam, where the discontented, the downtrodden and the debtors gathered around him. Neither David or anyone else realized at the time that this was the first important step toward becoming King of Judah and Israel. He built himself the nucleus of a private army from the riffraff who had flocked to him, and with this tightly-disciplined, fiercely-loyal striking force, began the series of moves which eventually carried him to his capital of Judah at Hebron, then to Jerusalem, where he reigned as King of Judah and Israel, the most powerful and respected world figure during his lifetime. With wily skill, David welded his army into highly mobile commando teams.

David, a shrewd politician, saw to it that this private army was bound to him personally, not to a locale, not to a group, nor even to a religious institution.

An army, however, needs supplies. As soon as David's commando force began to try to live off the land, it ran into trouble from local landowners. Although David's army was honing its fighting skills by taking on Philistine patrols near Keilah, some of the people near Keilah reported David's whereabouts to Saul. Saul came storming down to Keilah with a horde of heavily-armed troops, and David and his men fled to the wilderness of Ziph. Informers at Ziph, however, betrayed David's hiding place to Saul, and David was forced to retreat into rocky desert wadis south of Ziph.

Saul continued his manhunt. Through some of the most forbidding country anywhere in the world, where the temperatures climb to 120 degrees Fahrenheit, amid dizzying cliffs dropping into the deep trough, the Arabah, running from the Dead Sea down to the Gulf of Aqabah—the lowest place on the earth—Saul relentlessly tried to track down and murder David.

There were hairbreadth escapes. One time, David's group found itself almost in the clutches of Saul's overwhelming forces, when an emergency message about an invasion back home forced Saul to call off his men and turn back immediately. There was almost no pause, however; Saul soon returned to resume the deadly game. Although David took refuge in the remote caves above the Dead Sea near Engedi, Saul's remarkable secret police security apparatus got word of the new hiding place.

In spite of the constant danger and pressures, David preserved both a sense of honor and a sense of humor. One day, crouched far back in the fastnesses of a deep cave, trying to hide from Saul's killers, David was astonished to see the king himself crawl into the cave. David waited, holding his breath. He watched the king approach, then stop. Then David saw that Saul had entered the cave to answer the call of nature and had not realized that David lay there in hiding. While Saul was indisposed, David silently pulled out his sword. The young outlaw paused. It was so tempting to plunge the blade into the back of the temporarily helpless king.

One powerful thrust, and David's troubles could have ended immediately. Instead, he silently sliced off the tail of Saul's garment!

David waited until the king left the cave and started to walk down the mountainside. Holding aloft the piece of material cut from Saul's clothing, he called to Saul. David told the monarch that although he could have killed Saul, he had not and would not.

Saul, profoundly shaken by David's magnanimity, broke down. He tearfully addressed David as "my son," just as he had in the old days, and promised never again to threaten David.

As Saul and his army turned toward home, David sighed with relief. He soon learned, however, that Saul had quickly forgotten his kindness. David and his men found themselves on the run once again, desperately evading Saul's heavily armed hordes.

One night, David and a companion daringly slipped into Saul's camp. Eluding the sentries, the two came upon the sleeping king. David's comrade waited for David to pin Saul to the ground with one swift spear thrust—and end the dangerous cat-and-mouse game.

David knew how easy it would be to murder the unsuspecting king. He refused, however, to stoop to Saul's level of cruelty.

Instead, he prankishly picked up Saul's weapon and canteen and sneaked out of the camp. The following day, David trailed Saul's troops, until they came to a deep chasm. Shouting across the ravine from one side to the other at Saul and his staff, David showed the astonished king the spear and water bottle and playfully taunted Saul's guards for sleeping on duty. Then, in a serious vein, David addressed Saul, ". . . the Lord gave you into my hand today, and I would not put forth my hand against the Lord's anointed. Behold, as your life was precious this day in my sight, so may my life be precious in the sight of the Lord . . ." (26:24).

Although Saul had acted as an enemy, David remembered him as one who was precious in his sight because he knew that his own life—and every human life—was precious in the sight of the Lord. David knew that although God could choose to smash us in retaliation for what we do to Him, He spares us, using His power to restore the relationship between Him and us. This had become the dynamic for David's relationships with others. And it was more than pious talk. On two occasions, David had Saul within his grasp but spared him.

Although Saul again wept with remorse and acknowledged what a wretched, vengeful weakling he'd been, David suspected that the moment would pass. By this time, David had had enough narrow escapes. Existence in the wilderness was draining him of all ambition. He was beginning to desire merely to survive, if possible.

Surmising that Saul would return to take up the manhunt as on previous occasions, David and his private army turned again to the Philistines at Gath. It was a dangerous game, but it was even riskier to remain in Saul's territory. David by that time had a well-seasoned force of six hundred veterans. Until going to the Philistines, David had been the leader of rootless freebooters. Under Achish, the Philistine king of Gath, David started his political career. David was assigned a piece of territory with the understanding that his forces would not make trouble for Achish and would ward off marauding desert raiders. David and his six hundred settled in Ziklag, a grubby little village southeast of Beersheba, where David at last had his own domain.

One day, David received a summons from Achish to report with his six hundred men. David marched his men over the hot wastelands to honor his commitment to Achish. When David arrived, however, he and his men were miffed to learn that other Philistines regarded them as dubious allies. Ordered to return to Ziklag, David dutifully started to lead his private army home.

His troops, however, were disgruntled over not being permitted to share in the battle and plunder. Tired after a long, hot march to Jezreel and back without booty or honors, David's men were driven into frenzy of grief and anger when they approached Ziklag. The town had been raided and destroyed during their absence. Their wives, children and possessions had been carried away! Every man in the army, David included, had lost everything—youngsters and loved ones, personal property and wealth. The crushing sense of grief unleashed every kind of emotion.

For David, the worst hurt was the outburst against him. Many of his men blamed him for the disaster, bitterly denouncing his leadership. Some even muttered mutinously, threatening to stone him. David's weary journey through his personal wilderness reached its low point that day.

At a time when other young men would have quit in disgust, however, David ". . . strengthened himself in the Lord his God" (30:7).

The assurance of God may seem to the scoffer to be disgustingly frail stuff to march on. To David, however, it was the call to battle stations.

Calling his tired and mourning troops together, David proposed leaving immediately to pursue the invaders. The six hundred wiped their tears away, wearily buckled on their swords and filed out of the smoking ruins behind their young, indefatigable leader. By midafternoon when they came to the Besor brook, two hundred were too exhausted to continue the pursuit. David, however, roused the other four hundred to press on with him. Fortuitously, they ran across a sick Egyptian slaveboy, abandoned by his owner, who had been part of the Amalekite group which had raided Ziklag. David learned that the raiders were not far ahead. David's men successfully surprised the Amalekites at dusk, just as the camp was settling down for the night. Happily, all of David's forces' wives and children were alive and safe. David's men routed the Amalekites, released the captives, recovered all of their lost goods, and captured an enormous amount of booty.

Remarkably unselfish, David insisted that the four hundred share the loot with the two hundred who had been too exhausted to cross the Besor. David pointed out that those who stayed behind to guard the baggage had been serving as well as those in the front lines, recognizing the contribution of the unheralded heroes in life. The man who had been cursed a few hours earlier heard cheers from the same men. David sensed that he had won the hearts of his men for keeps.

Undisputed master of southern Judah and still in his twenties, David now knew for a certainty that he would eventually be king.

The one-time shepherd boy who felt that he was anointed by God realized that God always keeps His promises!

8
The Rebel

A FIFTEEN-YEAR-OLD boy from a fine home in an upper-class sub-urb was picked up by the police for car stripping. Head down, the youngster sat sullenly as his well-dressed parents badgered him with questions, such as, "Why did you break the law? What got into you, Jim?" Finally, the boy raised his head defiantly and blurted, "Well, what about all those souvenirs like towels and stuff that you bring home from motels after a business trip, Dad, and how about the way you laugh to your friends about the way you pad your expense account?"

George Eliot's lines in *Romola* remind us that "Our deeds are like children that are born to us; they live and act apart from our own will. Nay, children may be strangled, but deeds never; they have an indestructable life both in and out of our consciousness."

David discovered this. His adulterous affair with Bathsheba caused a chain reaction of domestic woes. Within his own family circle, as a result of the Bathsheba episode, David witnessed nearly every variety of shame and evil, including rape, murder, and civil war.

Among David's sons, the most spectacularly gifted and most like David was Absalom. Absalom, with a sleek, tiger beauty, strode with a stately, compelling flair. He was every inch the prince, exuding the royalty bestowed on him by both his father,

David, and his mother, Maacah, daughter of a king. ". . . in all
Israel, there was none so much to be praised for his beauty as
Absalom, from the sole of his foot to the crown of his head, there
was no blemish in him" (2 Samuel 14:25). Absalom's appearance
was enhanced by his hair, an enormous flowing mane. The boy soon
learned that his luxuriant crown of hair caused heads to turn in
admiration, and became vain about his coiffure.

David doted on Absalom. David, preoccupied with affairs of
state, however, gave little attention to being a father. Occasionally
looking at Absalom, his older half-brother Amnon, and his other
growing boys in a detached, sentimental way, David had only an
idealized picture of who they actually were. There were few re-
straints. David alternately ignored and indulged his sons. He
tolerated the atmosphere of intrigue and indolence, luxury and lust
in which his children were raised. There were delayed intentions
and postponed attentions: "Some day, I'll take time to have a
long talk with the boys; I must do some things with Absalom and
Amnon and the others." Meanwhile, Absalom, Amnon and the
other sons developed from toddlers to men before David had an
opportunity to know them. David saw Absalom and Amnon, not as
sons, but as strangers in his own household. As a ruler, David was
a success; he built a solid, powerful kingdom. As a father, however, he was a failure, building a flimsy, tenuous relationship with
Absalom and his other children.

Psychiatrists have frequently commented on the emotional dam-
age done to teen-age sons who discover that their fathers have been
running around with other women. Absalom and Amnon, David's
sons, are a classic case study.

Amnon, taking his cue from his father's lust, became infatuated
over his attractive half-sister, Tamar, who was Absalom's full
sister, and forced the girl to compromise herself, publicly shaming
her. Amnon, who deserved severest punishment, did not even receive a mild reprimand.

David, obsessed with his own guilt after his affair with Bathsheba, weakly stood by. Knowing that his own corrupt behavior
had already nullified anything he could say or do to correct
Amnon, he could not bring himself to reprove his eldest son.

Absalom was furious. Irate at his half-brother, Amnon, for violating Tamar, and angry at his father, David, for not exercising any authority or discipline, Absalom seethed with rage. He brooded over the situation for two years. He told and retold himself and a few cronies how indignant he was over the affront to his sister and how necessary it was to punish her wrongdoer to save her honor. His twisted chivalry, however, was a cover for his rage toward Amnon and David. Rekindling his anger toward Amnon and David every time he thought about the episode, feeding his growing grudge with additional slights, real or imagined, Absalom slowly began to build a plot. Meanwhile, the estrangement between Absalom and the rest of the family deepened.

Absalom's plot reflected the cunning of a killer wolf. Arranging with hired henchmen to murder Amnon at a prearranged signal, Absalom invited Amnon and his other half-brothers to a sheepshearing festival at his country place. The wine flowed freely; Amnon, duped into enjoying the party, had drunk too much to resist when Absalom gave the signal.

The other brothers had already suspected Absalom of ambitions to take over the throne. It was common in Oriental politics for one brother to kill off rival brothers to become king. Absalom's brothers, fearful of a possible bloodbath and aware of Absalom's brooding passion for revenge and preeminence, scattered. The first reports of the wild night to get back to David were rumors that Absalom had dispatched all of David's sons and proclaimed himself king. Although the correct story soon reached David, the king, crippled with self-accusation, collapsed in grief.

Absalom fled to his mother's people, and lived with his grandfather, Talmai, a king or tribal sheik in Geshur near Syria. With Amnon dead, Absalom knew that he was the heir to David's kingdom. Absalom waited for a message to return home, confident that after a suitable period of mourning for Amnon, David would realize that Absalom was the crown prince. Three years passed. Absalom fidgeted, and wondered about his father. The youth, beneath his swagger and sensuality, desperately longed for a father's love.

David, the father, meanwhile was immobilized by his ambivalent feelings toward this son so much like him. David saw in Absalom so much of the David he once was. Thinking of Absalom was like looking in a mirror thirty years earlier. All the memories of David's own youth were wakened. David noted that Absalom had so many of the qualities which had singled out him at Absalom's age: powerful, dashing, imaginative, electrically alive. David and Absalom, with so many gifts and traits in common, found themselves bound in a peculiarly tight love-hate relationship. David, so like his son in many ways, knew too well the mean and unpleasant character traits as well as the laudable in Absalom. Resenting and disliking the unlovely qualities of his own personality in Absalom, David could not bring himself to accept completely his own son.

David was simultaneously frightened and fascinated by the virile, winsome, dynamic youngster. Like any father, David was anxious to have Absalom succeed and yet was uneasy that Absalom would supplant him. David could not bring himself to think of stepping aside for the next generation. Caught in the crisis of middle-age, David knew that his own death was a certainty, his own powers were waning, his own mistakes were unerasable. He wanted—and did not want—to accept his own descent and his son's ascent. David found himself a near-irrational victim of competition with his own son. Although ". . . the king longed to go forth to Absalom . . ." (13:39), he did not. Emotionally locked in neutral, David remained in Jerusalem, out of contact with his favorite son.

The listless king was finally shaken out of his torpor by his tough, no-nonsense general Joab, and persuaded to permit Absalom to return to Jerusalem. When Absalom joyfully returned, David, withdrawn and secluded, made no effort to welcome the son. ". . . Let him dwell apart in his own house," the king ordered; "he is not to come into my presence . . ." (14:24). There was no reconciliation. David's invitation to the wayward son had strings attached. In fact, father and son did not see each other for two years after Absalom's return to Jerusalem.

It was not that Absalom wanted it that way. He repeatedly tried to get an audience with his father. Absalom could not even get an interview with Joab, David's general, until he resorted to setting fire to Joab's barley field as a device to make Joab see him. Absalom finally persuaded Joab to intercede for him. After five years —three years as a fugitive in Geshur and two years in Jerusalem after his return—Absalom finally managed to see David, his father.

The meeting was stiff and correct. As was proper, Absalom obediently prostrated himself—a sign of filial submission. David observed the proprieties, acknowledging the greeting, but showing no intention of restoring relations. It was face-saving ceremonial, primarily staged for the public. The breach had not been healed. At least this was the way that Absalom felt.

Absalom's affection for his father had been eroded by David's neglect. Even if David's kiss of greeting at the meeting was sincere, it was too late. The previous snubs over five years had alienated Absalom.

Smarting from the sting of parental indifference, Absalom grew more critical of his father. And there was plenty to criticize. King David, no longer the ruddy-faced shepherd boy who strummed a harp and composed lyrics to God, had declined into middle-aged slump. The sagging old lion seemed disinterested in the affairs of his kingdom. Depressed over his affair with Bathsheba which had sowed such a wind, David seemed resigned to reaping the whirlwind. Meanwhile, the nation drifted aimlessly. The kingdom, like David himself, seemed dull, tired and gray.

Absalom, acutely aware of his father's shortcomings, was totally unaware of his own. Never tormented by any self-doubt—as most stable leaders are on occasion—Absalom began to view himself as the country's charismatic deliverer.

With all the wiliness of a modern ward politician, Absalom appealed to the interests of his constituents. He mastered the arts of the office-seeker. He flattered. He promised. He listened sympathetically. He was accessible. He played on the incumbent's mistakes. He assured everyone that he'd do a superb job.

Perhaps most important for Absalom, he stirred peoples' imaginations, he exuded a vote-geting excitement. He seemed to possess that rare, indefinable quality which makes tired, hungry men cheer and charge back to battle, that elusive personal magnetism which propels a man to being captain of the team, president of the class.

Furthermore, his personal life style caught the nation's fancy. Who else drove dashingly through Jerusalem's streets in a flashy chariot pulled by horses, preceded by a colorfully-uniformed personal bodyguard of fifty cheering men? Who but Absalom could at the same time exhibit a hearty equalitarianism and interest in the ordinary peasant? Debonair Absalom, jumping out of his chariot, would move through the admiring crowds, pausing occasionally to talk with an ordinary peasant. When anyone started to bow in homage, he would grasp him as a brother. Absalom, the aristocrat with the common touch! Everything about him had a magnificence —his hair, his chariot, his guards, his rubbing shoulders with the plain folks in the market. And the people loved it!

Absalom, delighted with the attention given by the crowds he had been so long denied by his father, could not drink in enough of the cheers and comments. His craving for popularity was unsatiated by his chariot rides through the adoring populace day after day. He studied other ways to grab hurrahs and headlines.

Absalom's master stroke was to post himself prominently at the main gate of the city each morning when the heaviest traffic passed. He greeted the peasants carrying produce to the marketplaces, jovially bantering with them and solicitously inquiring about their problems. It was flattering to have the king's son being so attentive and asking such questions. When anyone approached with a grievance, no matter how trivial, Absalom feigned interest, agreed with the complaint wholeheartedly, regardless of the merits of the case. Absalom eagerly listened to all the petty gripes. At the same time, he shrewdly noted the comments reflected how creaky and bureaucratized David's kingdom had become. The winsome crowd pleaser encouraged the disaffected to think that if he were ruler, he'd solve their problems. He drank in the growing number of heady comments that the kingdom would be run a lot better if a man as sympathetic as Absalom were in power.

His grandstanding ". . . stole the hearts of the men of Israel" (15:6). Who could fail to admire this affable, agreeable young prince? After four years, his splashy gestures won him wide support.

Absalom by that time had totally convinced himself of two things: (1) his father, David, was the cause of every problem, personal or national; (2) he, Absalom, could remedy everything. Absalom, resentful of David's authority, grew increasingly willing to challenge his father. His dreams untempered by experience, the young man thought with the cocky, restless self-confidence of a man with no yesterdays but many tomorrows. Surrounded by admirers, he fancied himself as the man who could restore a vigor and tone to the flabby, sluggish government.

Absalom had one fatal flaw. He had no corrective to his own thoughts, no yardstick beyond his own whims. There was nothing to refine his ambitions. He could persuade himself that whatever he wanted was proper. Self-centered and self-sufficient, he was, in spite of personal attractiveness and charisma, doomed to be one more frustrated reformer-conqueror. In brief, Absalom's problem was that he was a practicing atheist. He had no consciousness of God, therefore, he was obedient only to his own impulses. His universe, like his luxuriant hairdo, was rooted in Absalom's head. Both existed for Absalom's glory; both could be combed and controlled to his advantage. As a symbol of his arrogant self-esteem, Absalom built for himself a lavish, ornate mausoleum where he intended to be buried, confident of his memory being perpetuated for all time.

It was not difficult to organize an underground movement. Absalom unearthed many pockets of one-time Saul supporters who had resented David through the years. Others, the youth knew, were disenchanted with David and wanted a change. Absalom's *élan* attracted the glory-seekers, the fed-up, the malcontents, the disaffected, the slighted, the incensed. The young prince and would-be usurper organized them into a tightly-disciplined cadre.

Absalom's coup was bold and imaginative. His well-trained organization fanned out to key locations. When the signal was given throughout the country, they were instructed to shout, *"Absalom is king!"*

Appropriately, he selected Hebron as the place to light the fuse, remembering that it was the city in which David had opened his reign. Hebron was also a hotbed of unhappy subjects who had never forgiven David for transferring his capital from their city. Furthermore, Hebron was strategically a good site for a retreat into the wilderness in event of reverses.

In case David's police were keeping Absalom under surveillance, Absalom cunningly prepared a ruse to leave Jerusalem and go to Hebron. He played on his father's religious sensitivities, telling the old man that he wanted to go to Hebron for an act of worship. Absalom had no reluctance to using the name of God when it suited. Like many politicians, he was prepared to exploit the Lord, if it advanced the campaign. His veneer of piety convinced David and impressed Jerusalem. Two hundred unsuspecting leading figures agreed to accompany Absalom to Hebron.

Absalom intended to manipulate the two hundred leading lights into appearing to be backers of the conspiracy, figuring that others would join him when they saw such distinguished citizens in his retinue. Absalom also counted on the tinder of discontent among his father's subjects to ignite instantly into a blaze of support once the coup at Hebron was announced.

The timing was perfect. The two hundred unwittingly lent respect and support to the young man's plot. The underground in key cities throughout the kingdom rose up and shouted that Absalom was king. Absalom assumed that there would be such a spontaneous outpouring of support that David would be forced aside. Confidently planning his victory march through Jerusalem, Absalom moved toward the capital without opposition, expecting to pick up the reins of government. He believed the enthusiastic claque following him which assured him that the kingdom was his. His gamble apparently paid off; resistance melted as his cause gained momentum. Important people joined up, such as David's chief counselor, Ahithophel (who as Bathsheba's grandfather was undoubtedly still incensed over the blotch David had brought on the family honor).

David, afraid of additional treachery in Jerusalem, fled. Accompanied only by a few companies of trusted veterans from the old days and some mercenaries, the dispirited old man moved toward the Jordan valley, which seemed to have a higher concentration of loyal subjects.

Absalom marched into the abandoned capital. He strutted through the streets, acknowledging the cheers, then moved into the royal palace. His first act was significant. He took over the royal harem, displacing David and symbolizing the total and deliberate break with his father. All the ties were now cut. The harem episode, the grossest, most irreparable insult to David possible in the Middle East, marked the point of no-return in the revolution. The populace and particularly any wavering followers were forced by the harem take-over to choose sides.

At the same time, Absalom turned into a playboy. Instead of taking immediate steps to consolidate his position by a search-and-destroy campaign against David and his loyalists, thereby eliminating any threat of David returning, Absalom romped with the harem girls.

David had only two ace cards, and he played them well. One was the loyalty of a cold but cagey military strategist named Joab. The other was the services of a clever genius named Hushai who agreed to stay in Jerusalem to head David's spy apparatus and espionage efforts.

As Absalom lounged indolently in Jerusalem, David slowly rallied. Enough of the old fire remained in the ashes of his character to inspire loyalty. Ahithophel, David's counselor who had defected to Absalom, realized that David would try a comeback. Ahithophel sensibly urged Absalom to mount a lightning thrust into the Jordan valley, assassinate David, scatter his troops, demoralize his followers and woo back loyalists with promises of peace and amnesty.

Absalom, however, wavered. Instead of striking out immediately, he listened to Hushai, David's secret agent. Absalom was both frightened and flattered by Hushai's words. Absalom grew alarmed at Hushai's exaggerated description of David's forces, pictured as an enraged she-bear lurking in ambush, ready to pounce on the rebels. Uneasily, Absalom imagined that he was up against a superfoe. The rest of Hushai's advice appealed to Absalom: Mobilize a mighty standing army of thousands who will throng to join the cause, then like a great tide wipe out any opposition. In Absalom's mind there was the fascinating picture of himself at the head of an enormous conquering army. His vanity got the better of his common sense.

Absalom leisurely gathered an army. Foolishly, he put a young fop named Amasa in charge—a man with little military experience whose main credentials were that he had married the daughter of Absalom's first cousin. The huge but ill-trained army moved out of Jerusalem in a holiday mood. Buoyed by the easy successes of the Jerusalem takeover, the usurper and his followers recklessly attacked.

David's general, Joab, had carefully deployed his seasoned but out-numbered loyalist troops so that Absalom's attackers would be maneuvered into the forest of Ephraim. Joab correctly decided that if Absalom and his hordes could be lured into the forest, they could be separated, confused and destroyed piecemeal.

David, Absalom's father, knowing that his leaders had out-generaled his son, realized that they would isolate Absalom from his huge mob-army and snare him. ". . . Deal gently for my sake with the young man Absalom," David plaintively pleaded (18:5). David suspected that his hardboiled guards would show little mercy—and beneath the royal robes, there still beat a father's heart.

Joab's strategy worked perfectly. It was a total disaster for Absalom's swarm of inexperienced revolutionaries. Rebel units were broken up in the thick woods. Absalom's men, separated from leaders, were ambushed by Joab's steely regulars. Hundreds wandered through the underbrush, confused and lost. A cautious retreat quickly erupted into a complete rout.

Absalom, unable to rally his panicky troops, saw that it was an every-man-for-himself effort to escape, and took off by himself. Galloping along a forest path on his mule, he encountered a detachment of loyalists. He quickly turned and headed his mule into the woods. Apparently looking back to see if he was being pursued, he didn't see the two low-hanging branches. Absalom rode with such speed that the force of the forward motion jammed his neck in a vise-grip between the branches, leaving him dangling helplessly several feet off the ground as the mule dashed on, and entangling his hair in the thicket of prickly branches. He struggled frantically, attempting desperately to pry apart the two heavy branches, squirming and kicking to try to get his feet on some solid support to take the weight of his body off his neck and head, and bellowing for his attendants.

David's awe-struck soldiers quickly surrounded the prince but shrank from attacking. Grimly-efficient Joab rode up and with the same cold detachment he'd use in killing a snake hurled three javelins at the writhing, puppetlike figure suspended from the branches, badly wounding Absalom. Against David's orders, Joab cold-bloodedly ordered the rebel prince cut down and executed on the spot.

The historian who wrote 2 Samuel was struck with the ludicrous fact that one of the main sources of Absalom's vainty, his hair, should have contributed to his downfall. It seemed ironic that the symbol of Absalom's pride should have trapped him in a deadly way, and the object lesson still stands today.

The final note of irony in Absalom's meteoric rise and fall was his burial. Although he had conceitedly prepared a costly funeral tomb for himself, confident that he'd be revered even in death and honored by subsequent generations, Absalom's corpse was dragged to a pit in the woods and unceremoniously dumped. As a gesture of disrespect and disgust, David's soldiers filed by and tossed rocks at the body until a large stone heap covered the carcass. The impressive mausoleum was never used; the dramatic state funeral was never held; the odes to Absalom's memory were never sung. Some young men struggle into oblivion.

The only one to mourn for Absalom was his father, David. He sobbed, ". . . O my son Absalom, my son, my son, Absalom! Would I had died instead of you, O Absalom, my son, my son!" (18:33). David's desperate cry was from one who had to live with memories, from a parent who'd lost his son long before he entered the battle in Ephraim woods. Son and father had drifted farther and farther apart, neither finally able to close the breach that led to the death of one. David lived on, but could measure his life only in terms of his loss.

Every father should know that there are many ways to lose his son. And every son should know that there are many ways to lose a

father. Relationships are so precarious, so fragile. Mutual acceptance starts with accepting the Father's acceptance. There is life-
giving news for every fumbling, insensitive son and father of every
generation. Through the Cross and Resurrection, God confers the
new standing of *forgiven* sinner on every modern Absalom-David
combination!

Elihu

9

The Ideologist

HIS VERY NAME, Elihu, meaning *He is my God,* conveyed the set jaw of a young man determined to be religious. Serious and unsmiling, Elihu prided himself on being theologically precise. He had memorized the creed. He had learned the correct vocabulary. For every theological question, he had cross-indexed the catechism answers. Young Elihu, like a well-read religion-philosophy major, held the proper textbook faith. Cocky, bright, and inflexible, Elihu, in spite of his youth, considered himself an authority on religion.

Elihu's religion, however, was the rigid orthodoxy of a young man secretly afraid that the least breeze of doubt would blow over his fragile toothpick castle of beliefs. He had stacked up a system of solutions, all developed with careful logic from a sophisticated, cerebral notion of the Almighty.

When he heard about the misfortunes of a distant kinsman, Job (both were descended from Nahor, Abraham's brother), Elihu thought that Job would be an interesting case study. Elihu knew the details of Job's tragedies: all of his great wealth lost, his vast and valuable herds of she-asses and camels seized by desert raiders or killed by lightning; all of his offspring (the eldest still an unmarried youngster) wiped out suddenly when a building collapsed on them during a horrible hurricane; Job's youthful vigor (Job is described fourteen times in *Job* as a strong man in the prime of life) destroyed by a gruesome disease in which painful, oozing, never-healing sores broke out everywhere, even in his throat, causing him to choke in his sleep and to have horrible nightmares. Elihu knew that Job had not only lost everything, with no possible chance of making a fresh start, but was enduring such humiliations as no longer enjoying the privilege of having older men get up in his presence in recognition of his wealth and power. Furthermore, Elihu had heard that Job's disease was incurable and that Job was dying.

The young theologian was curious how his relative Job was accepting tragedy. Most important, Elihu was anxious to share his abundant store of religious answers. Elihu visited Job.

When he arrived, however, Elihu found that three older men, Eliphaz, Bildad, and Zophar, had also come. He listened in silence to the windy, tedious sermons from the three friends, champions of conventional religion. Growing impatient as the friends droned on, Elihu noted that their arguments about divine justice failed to move Job. To everyone's annoyance, Job defiantly shouted, "Not guilty!" not once but seventeen different times. Elihu barely contained himself during three repetitious rounds of speeches by Eliphaz, Bildad, and Zophar and grew increasingly irked when no one of the trio gave an answer to silence Job.

Elihu finally jumped in. Like the Sunday school class which adopted as its motto, COURAGE, LORD, WE ARE COMING! he stepped up as God's champion, determined to get Him out of a tight fix. Disappointed that the older men had not upheld God's reputation nor put Job in his place, Elihu decided to set things right. He had waited and waited. Now he would say his piece.

". . . I am full of words . . ." (Job 32:18), the original Mr. Answer Man bubbled. Cocky and self-righteous, Elihu implied that he had a private, hot line to the Almighty and held more insights than the three older comforters-advisers. Pretentiously claiming the gift of "the breath of the Almighty" (32:8) which gave him exceptional understanding, Elihu observed, "It is not the old that are wise . . ." and commanded, ". . . Listen to me; let me also declare my opinion" (32:8–10). The young man, preening himself on his profound thought, appointed himself seminar leader.

Elihu put down Job, sniffing ". . . be silent, and I will teach you wisdom" (33:33).

Elihu then took Job to task for charging God with not answering Job's questions. Incensed that Job should claim to be innocent, he berated Job for asking God for reasons for his woes.

With the smooth self-assurance of the man who has read all the books on pain but never felt any hurt, young Elihu accused Job of blasphemy. Job had asked for a day in court, for a hearing. Who can dare question God? Elihu huffed.

For all his overbearing self-assurance, Elihu's speeches had their good points. He doggedly guarded God's sovereignty. No watery humanism for Elihu! Intensely God-directed, Elihu insisted God be given preeminence. He would not stand for anyone's trying to lay down conditions for the Almighty. He would not permit God's prerogatives to be grabbed by any mortal. "Will he then make requital to suit you, because you reject it . . .?" (34:33). Elihu correctly pointed out that God is not accountable to Job or anyone.

Furthermore Elihu stated that a person must seek God for his own sake, not as a gimmick. He abhorred the notion that God is a flunky, a tool to be used to get something better than God. Elihu pleaded for man to cry, "Where is God my Maker, who gives songs in the night?" (35:10).

The young man, determined to keep God, not man, at the center, recoiled from the type of religion which allows a blurry deity to become eclipsed by man.

Moreover, Elihu had deep insights on the nature of sin. He correctly asserted that no man may play cute games with God. No passive, motionless Buddhist divinity for Elihu! His God moves, reacts, vibrates with terrible activity. Elihu asserted that man stands accountable constantly.

Elihu rightly emphasized that no man deserves anything from God. No person can make any claim on Him. Elihu, however, pushed his point to where his God sounded disturbingly similar to a Moslem's description of Allah, an awesome, all-powerful Deity who passes out rewards and punishments. "God is clothed with terrible majesty," he pontificated. "The Almighty—we cannot find Him; He is great in power and justice (37:22–23).

Elihu's logic got the best of him. He ended up with a ledgerbook-God who must constantly settle all accounts and mete out immediate penalties. "He does not keep the wicked alive but gives the afflicted their right" (36:6), Elihu asserted, adding, "If they hearken and serve him, they complete their days in prosperity and their years in pleasantness. But if they do not hearken, they perish by the sword, and die without knowledge" (36:11–12).

These are the conclusions of a grim legalist. Elihu's idea of God finally became an extension of his own censorious personality. Elihu revealed that he had never been broken and put together again by grace. He never thought in terms of mercy because he had never had to beg for it, had never received it, nor ever granted it. Elihu was so self-sufficient that he really needed no God. For all his lofty truisms about divine sovereignty, Elihu's picture of The Other was merely that of a celestial accountant.

Apart from God's own disclosure of Himself, we end up with one-sided views of God's nature. Our own home-brewed "God" will usually either be a Tyrant or a Tabby, man's oppressor or man's pet.

Elihu never grasped the meaning of the mystery of human suffering. Job, on the other hand, had tried to understand suffering. Job had never tried to pose as a paragon of virtue. Job had even been willing to acknowledge his guilt. But he could not accept the notion that God was out to pay him back for secret heinous crimes. He simply refused to believe that his horrible misfortunes implied drastic punishment for monstrous offenses.

It never occurred to Elihu to consider that the righteous as well as the wicked suffer. The good man as well as the evil may lose children, encounter reverses, weep with pain, deteriorate with disease.

Elihu, with the facile armchair-philosophizing of a youthful thinker who has not yet learned that some pain is stupid and senseless, offered such trite moralisms as: "Suffering develops your character"; "God clobbers a man to keep him in line"; "Whatever happens is all for the best."

Job must neither expect mercy nor ask it of God, Elihu preached. Any hopes of forgiveness were presumptuous. Furthermore, he informed Job, if God wants to torture His subjects, He may. And no one is to murmur or complain. Job's sufferings, Elihu made clear, were because Job needed to be chastised. According to Elihu, Job had to suffer and shut up. God is not to be put on the witness stand; His verdicts are never to be questioned. Cold and cerebral, Elihu's entire goal was to shove Job into confessing and then converting him. Once Job owned up to his sins Elihu was certain that God would smile on Job and everything would end happily.

Reworking Churchill's memorable phrase about Russian foreign policy, we sigh that human suffering is like a puzzle locked in a riddle, wrapped in an enigma. In melancholy bewilderment, we conclude that our Kafka-esque existence is absurd and futile—until we are confronted by the Suffering God of the Cross and Emmaeus road. God shares and bears our sorrows! Better than answers to hard reality of suffering, we have Him Whose Presence is answer enough.

What Elihu thought was a theology was actually an ideology. And there is a difference between the two. Theology liberates; ideology confines. Theology is flexible, vital, creative. Ideology is rigid, dead, static. Theology is discovering how God continually springs His surprises on us. Ideology with dull predictability imposes a rigid system on others. Theology sings of responsible personhood before the Living One. Ideology manipulates and exploits others to fit them into molds. Theology is a process, fluid and alive, which energizes, enlivens. Ideology tries to structure everything. Ideology constricts and contains.

Ideologies abound today: capitalism and communism, conservatism and liberalism, Calvinism and Catholicism, Maoism and Marxism, the Playboy philosophy and Puritanism—not to mention the ideologies promulgated by Ayn Rand, the John Birch Society, K K K, the S D S, the A D A, the New Left, the Panthers, the pronouncement portfolio from the home office of most name-brand denominations.

Uncritical acceptance of any ideology means giving ultimate

value to a man-made system. The Biblical message warns against this insidious form of idolatry. God alone can claim ultimate value.

Elihu, tyrannized by the ideology of suffering-means-punishment, lived a religious charade. Arrogantly self-righteous, he squashed dissent. Elihu, like every ideologist, was intolerant. He was threatened by any doubts, was blind to other viewpoints. Making absolutes of partial truths, Elihu the religious ideologist opposed any questioner.

Elihu's gloomy ideological pretensions never experienced the sunburst of energizing judgment-mercy. Consequently, he constantly tried to structure and contain Job in the Elihu ideology. *Elihuism* was what this young man wanted to defend. For all his passion for God's honor and God's sovereignty, Elihu's real religion focused on his own little pet scheme of divine retribution.

Religious ideology is theology-gone-rancid, an *idea* of God replacing *obedience* to God. Young Elihu, in Mark Twain's biting phrase, was a *good* man in the worst sense of the word!

For all his lofty thoughts about God, Elihu never had a concern about Job as a hurting, lonely man. Refuting all of Job's arguments, he never saw the arguer. Although he was correctly orthodox in his religious ideology, Elihu, however, showed no sympathy, no warmth, no compassion. The youthful philosopher never grasped that Job needed a friend, not explanations.

Job's problem was existential, not ideological. Job, tormented in his suffering, struggled to live. In that desperate struggle, skepticism was sometimes close to believing, scoffing to affirming.

Elihu, however, had to apply his little ideology like a mold, and press Job into it. He could not accept Job as a person. Elihu heard only the blasphemous rhetoric, never listening to the aching cry of the man Job caught in the mystery of suffering. With a prissy self-righteousness, Elihu determined to have Job use the safe, sanitized Sunday-school jargon of conventional piety before he would accept him. Elihu, who had never known many hurts, could not comprehend Job's misery or rage.

Business executives, tests show, spend 80 percent of their time listening to people, yet don't hear half of what is said. Consequently, special courses in listening have been devised.

We, like Elihu, hear but do not listen to the hurting Job beside us. We must struggle to hear the hurting human behind the words.

One of the astonishing aspects of Jesus' life was His ability to hear other people. In spite of the interruptions in His crowded schedule and in spite of the pettiness of many of the requests, Jesus inevitably listened. Others dismissed these whining nuisances as beggars or lepers; Jesus always listened to the human behind the sounds He heard.

He has listened to the human cry behind the sounds of *our* loud curses, our elaborate speeches, our anguished shrieks. Jesus Christ is the Master Listener.

Like Elihu, we need to be sensitized to the cries of the Job sitting next to us. The more aware we are of Him who listens to us, the more aware we are of others.

10
The Misfit

SOMETIMES, an apparently intact society develops cracks, and, like a huge antique vase, suddenly breaks up. The scalpel-sharp edges of the broken pieces of a shattered culture lacerate—especially the psyches of the young.

Wishing to avoid the scratches, cuts and bleeding, many youths choose to opt out: through drugs hard and soft, by Eastern mysticism and escape cults, in a cave on Crete or a commune in the desert. Others, secretly cop-outs but outwardly straight, have privately given up on democracy, the Church, God, human existence, themselves. Tragically, other cop-outs are not so passive; suicide is the number-two cause of death among college students today.

Jeremiah was a would-be cop-out. He longed to get away from it all and retreat to a desert hideway, ". . . that I might leave my people and go away from them . . ." (Jeremiah 9:2).

This paradoxical figure of a prophet was the most reluctant spokesman for God in the Bible. The last thing Jeremiah wanted to be was a prophet. What he wanted more than anything was obscurity, and the security that obscurity brings.

He had no stomach for controversy. He disliked having to stir things up, even for God. He was God's man in spite of himself. In fact, he ranted and screamed at God. In his *Confessions* (which are inserted throughout the book of Jeremiah), Jeremiah's near-blasphemous dialogues with God show an intensity and honesty unmatched anywhere.

His call, for example, revealed a profound struggle between a young man in his early twenties (the meaning of the Hebrew word for *youth* used in 1:6) and God. Haltingly, Jeremiah recounted how he was grabbed by the God who won't take *no* for an answer.

> Before I formed you in the womb
> I knew you,
> and before you were born I conse-
> crated you!
> I appointed you a prophet to the
> nations. (1:5)

Although he knew that he was known even in prefetal state by the Knower and Former of his life, Jeremiah protested! He pleaded that he did not know how to speak, that he was too inexperienced and immature. He twisted and evaded; he balked and alibied.

God, however, will not be put off.

> Do not say, "I am only a youth";
> for to all to whom I send you you
> shall go. (1:6)

Once a person is ever awakened to the reality of the Knower, he knows that he will always be haunted with the troubling memory that he is claimed by God. That person will forever be under a compulsion because of the Compeller.

Although Jeremiah recorded that he was "touched" by God (1:9), he knew that he actually had been seized! In fact, it was more like being grabbed by the nape of the neck and tossed into the pit of national affairs. Jeremiah learned that God's confrontation with a person is seldom soul-warming ecstasy but usually a brusque command to get to work.

Furthermore, Jeremiah discovered that God's call is never in heavenly generalities, but always in earthly specifics. One of God's quirks, Jeremiah decided, is that God cares nothing for grandiose promises, but pushes His "called" into gritty particularity. "Go and proclaim in the hearing of Jerusalem," he understood the Lord to say (2:2).

Jerusalem! That was the last place in the world Jeremiah wanted to speak. He told himself that he was just a country boy from Anathoth, a little hick town a long hour's trip from the big city. Go to Jerusalem? Never, not that place, Jeremiah swore.

The young man had heard the stories of the seething capital. He knew how depraved the city had become under King Manasseh. Son of a priest descended from a leading family, Jeremiah had overheard the older folks discussing the way Judah had deteriorated morally under Manasseh. Jeremiah had personally seen some of Manasseh's efforts to introduce Assyrian customs in order to update Judah. He shuddered when he recalled some of these Assyrian practices such as child sacrifice and depraved fertility rites. A sensitive God-haunted boy, Jeremiah had noticed that Manasseh's hideous Assyrianization program had nearly eclipsed God-worship, even in a little out-of-the-way place like Anathoth. And he was supposed to spend his life in Jerusalem, the headquarters for all the organized crime and evil in the land? He hunted ways to evade going to Jerusalem to speak for God.

When he heard that King Manasseh had died and his son Josiah had come to the throne, young Jeremiah cheered wildly. He rejoiced, certain that everything would be well in Judah for years. He listened to Josiah's rhetoric and felt his pulse quicken. With thousands of his countrymen, the young man began to dream of independence for Judah. Nearly every night, he sat up late in the student gathering-places, singing freedom songs and entering into heady discussions about Judah's heritage under God.

When young King Josiah announced a clean-up program after some priests uncovered an ancient Law book (Deuteronomy) while repairing the long-neglected Temple, Jeremiah's hopes soared. At last, he told himself, Judah would recover its sense of obedience and mission as God's people! Jeremiah joined enthusiastically in the great public rallies. Endorsing Josiah's Judean

Reform Movement, he felt confident that a great new age had
dawned for Judah.

To smart, sensitive Jeremiah, however, there were soon some
disquieting aspects to Josiah's reform movement. For one thing,
most of the changes were either administrative or legislative
changes. Village shrines had been boarded up and religion cen-
tralized in the Jerusalem Temple. Reorganization, Jeremiah discovered, was not enough; new denominational apparatus and
different structures would not suffice. Nor would more laws. Jeremiah, perturbed that widows were still poor and orphans still oppressed, uneasily concluded that much of Josiah's reform effort
was on paper. The nation, he noted, had merely doffed its hat to
religion, then turned back to making money.

Unexpectedly, while Jeremiah was still in his teens, dashing
young King Josiah died in battle (608 B.C.). The sparkling reform
movement sputtered and stalled completely. The nation spiralled
downward. From the New Frontier under Josiah with its ask-not-
what-your-country-can-do-for-you vigor, Judah sank into a dismal
twilight of whining and wining. Jeremiah groaned when Josiah's
son, a greedy, incompetent egomaniac named Jehoiakim, was
crowned. King Jehoiakim, living in a dream world, stupidly allo-
cated enormous funds to build himself a lavish new palace. To
finance this costly showpiece, Jehoiakim levied crushing taxes on
the poor. Most people were diverted from thinking too much about
Jehoiakim's irresponsibility, however, because hated Assyria was
collapsing. There was singing in the streets over Assyria's dis-
integration. The old earthy gods of the erotic pagan cults began to
slink back.

Meanwhile, Jehoiakim's paid priests fostered a State Religion,
with dramatic mass rallies, colorful ceremonies, and numerous
unctuous prayers. Jehoiakim's Judah, drunk with religious nationalism, believed its myths that God held Judah as His favorite and
Jerusalem as the earthy seat of His rule. To question these myths
was not just bad manners; it was blasphemy and treason com-
bined.

It was not that there was no religion; it was because there was too much of the wrong kind of religion. Genuine religion on the visceral level was displaced by a flashy but phony piety-cum-nationalism. Service was replaced by ceremony; humility by *hubris;* mercy by moralism; justice by jingoism; sensitivity by superstition. Judah's faith became a heady mixture of prayer and patriotism, of praise-the-Lord-and-pass-the-ammunition. The Temple declined into a sort of Department of Religious Affairs under Judah's Foreign Office and Pentagon. God was assumed to be irrevocably committed to Judah's defense, and, to hear some talk, almost like Judah's pet watchdog.

Young and angry, Jeremiah saw issues in sharp focus. The sentimentalism of middle age had not begun to blur his view. And when Jeremiah spoke, he did not whisper. He shouted! His sermon in the Temple courtyard at Jerusalem (7:1–15), for example, still sizzles and blisters, and is hardly the refined address one expects of a budding young preacher.

In this Temple sermon he excoriated the religious establishment for reducing faith to slick slogans such as, ". . . This is the temple of the Lord, the temple of the Lord, the temple of the Lord" (7:3). Judah's religion was rancid, Jeremiah bellowed. The fancy Temple ceremonial was a cover-up for willful evildoing in daily life, and the Lord prefered a hearty heretic to a flabby phony!

Jeremiah concluded his first public sermon in Jerusalem with a sharp ultimatum. Unless Judah desisted from injustice and immorality, oppression and idolatry immediately, the young prophet warned, the Jerusalem Temple would meet the same fate as the ancient Shiloh sanctuary—destroyed by enemies!

Jeremiah had touched the sensitive nerve. He could not have possibly picked an issue which would have upset his hearers more. Everything about his maiden effort at preaching—his subject matter and his style of delivery—seemed designed to offend. By talking in these tones and words, especially in front of the sacred Temple and in those days, the young man alienated everyone.

The few friends who would still speak to him asked why he had chosen to attack the Temple. Did Jeremiah not remember that everything socially and religiously acceptable and approved centered on the official Temple religion?

Everyone else, especially the Religious Establishment, boiled angrily after hearing Jeremiah's stinging criticisms. The furious Temple priests and prophets tried to have the nation arrest and pass the death sentence on him. The backlash of resentment against young Jeremiah continued to swell.

Deeply shaken, he tried to maintain his equilibrium. He heard the rumors swirling through Jerusalem that some were plotting to kill him. One day, Jeremiah was accosted by a group from his hometown. At first he thought that they might have come to offer him some encouragement and support. He recognized them as cousins and friends he had known since childhood. Suddenly, he realized they smouldered with anger.

". . . Do not prophesy in the name of the Lord or you will die by our hand," they threatened him (11:22).

Surely, Jeremiah told himself after his long-time buddies left, they were just talking. He knew that they were hostile and frustrated, but he assured himself that they would simmer down.

A few days later, however, Jeremiah found himself waylaid by some of these same relatives and friends. He barely managed to escape alive.

This was getting to be too much, Jeremiah thought to himself. Being God's spokesman made him especially vulnerable. He felt deeply hurt that members of his family had tried to kill him. He struggled with himself to overcome his inclinations to get revenge. Remembering that he belonged to God, however, Jeremiah finally resolved to forgive them and give them another chance.

Jeremiah quickly discovered what his relatives and boyhood friends did with their second chance; they tried to murder him a second time!

Two assassination attempts—and by his own kin—broke Jeremiah's patience. How long would this have to go on? How would he survive?

The young prophet had had enough. He addressed the Lord. Trying to be polite, Jeremiah at first restrained himself. Finally, however, he could not hold back his resentment. "Why?" he spluttered, "Why does the way of the wicked prosper? Why do all who are treacherous thrive?" (12:1).

What's wrong with you, Lord? Jeremiah stormed. Can't you see what they're trying to do to me? Here I am, trying to do your work, and you let these so-and-so's try to kill me? How come?

God gave Jeremiah no baby talk. Instead of a lollipop and a there-there-now you-poor-little-fellow cheeriness, God roughly commanded Jeremiah to get ready to move out again. He was told that he hadn't seen anything yet. If he were tired from running against these men, what would he do when up against real competition? If he were sniffling because a bunch of small-town petty priests and relatives had gotten him down, wait until he encountered major-league adversaries, including King Jehoiakim himself!

"Don't let a couple of close shaves with death get you down," God in effect rumbled to the youth; "You've still got a long way to go with worse yet to come, Jeremiah."

Young Jeremiah's flabby spiritual muscles needed to be strengthened. His questions were not answered; rather, he was matured to hang on.

Faith is not assenting to facts about something; it is being gripped by Someone. Tough questions batter it; apparent puzzles such as, "Why do evil-doers apparently do so well?" bewilder us. With the God who knows and cares, however, the shafts of adversity become the reinforcing rods of character.

Jeremiah persevered. He loved his people and his country, Judah, but he loved justice more. He continued to speak out, denouncing the corruption and apostasy of Judah. Even the pagans, with all their misguided, counterfeit religions, at least were loyal to their fake gods. Not Judea, Jeremiah yelled. Obsessed with a sense of doom hanging over the nation, he reluctantly persisted in announcing to his countrymen that a day of reckoning was inevitable unless they drastically changed their hearts and life styles.

Assyria, which had been the hated overlord of Judah for nearly two hundred years, fell to the Babylonians four years after Josiah's death. Caught in the crunch so many times between the two world superpowers, Assyria and Egypt, Judah cheered. With Assyria gone and Egypt weakened, Judah thought she could return forever to the good old days of glory.

It was, of course, a fool's paradise. Judah's leaders flexed their nation's puny biceps, brazenly confident that God would inevitably bless them. Astonishingly, they refused to take seriously the new world colossus, Babylon. Judah, strategically located on key trade routes, could not dare to threaten Babylon. Judah arrogantly spurned Babylon's request to be a satellite state, confident that the Temple, the kingdom of Judah, prosperity and God's favor were here to stay forever and ever.

Jeremiah felt like weeping. He knew how chauvinistic the national policies had become. Outwardly, Jeremiah—the most detested man in Judah—appeared too brash and outspoken. Inwardly obsessed with a premonition of doom for the country he loved and a sense of ostracism from his family and friends, Jeremiah churned and wished he could evade his job as God's spokesman.

The prophet who wanted to cop out could not. Throughout his early manhood, he was hurting and hurting badly.

He spilled his feelings in remarkably candid dialogues with God. Certain passages of the book of Jeremiah, the prophet's *Confessions,* record the most intimate, intense God-man encounters known outside of Gethsemane.

"O Lord, thou hast duped me, and I have been thy dupe:" (20:7 NEB), young Jeremiah exploded on one occasion. Alternating between bouts of confident faith and all-is-hopeless weariness, Jeremiah was emotionally torn apart. He pleaded to be allowed to quit. Rebuffed, he angrily swore at God: "Cursed be the day on which I was born!" (20:14). Sometimes he sank to near-suicidal despair and berated the Lord for not aborting him before his birth: "Why," Jeremiah shouted at God, "did I come forth from the womb to see toil and sorrow, and spend my days in shame?" (20:18). Then he raged. Then he sobbed. Then he flung accusations at the Almighty. Bitterly, he denounced God: ". . . Thou art to me like a brook that is not to be trusted, whose waters fail . . ." (15:18 NEB).

Although he sometimes even damned God, Jeremiah had to conclude invariably, "If I say, 'I will not mention him or speak any more in his name,' there is in my heart as it were a burning fire shut up in my bones, and I am weary with holding it in, and I cannot" (20:9). Nowhere in human language is there a more apt description of the divinely-ignited, ever-smouldering compulsion to stand and speak for God.

His opponents continued to harass him. One day, outside Jerusalem, witnessed by several priests and a large crowd, Jeremiah smashed a large pottery jar, dramatically illustrating how God would use Babylon to destroy Judah. When he tried to enter the Temple grounds, he was arrested, humiliatingly locked up in stocks for the night, and forbidden ever to enter the Temple area again. Ostracized, plotted against, jeered at, Jeremiah nevertheless continued to puncture Judah's pretense and complacency by warning of dire days to come. So certain was he of the impending doom on Judah that he refused to marry and enjoy the comforts of family life.

With fire in his bones, Jeremiah brooded over his people's disobedience to God. What could bring them back? In 605 B.C., he made a last effort to appeal to his countrymen to wake up. He dictated a compendium, a boiled-down version of his earlier sermons, to a companion named Baruch. Forbidden to enter the Temple himself, Jeremiah sent Baruch to read the ultimatum from the Lord.

The scroll warned Judah that it was on a disaster course, that mighty Nebuchadnezzar's Babylon hordes would pour through the country, slaughtering, burning, pillaging, torturing and deporting the populace, unless the nation drastically changed. Hearing the seditious-sounding words being read to the public, the police hauled Baruch before Jehoiakim, who demanded to hear Jeremiah's latest outburst. As the irate king heard each section of the indicting scroll, he contemptuously took his penknife, sliced out the offending column and insultingly dropped it into the fire.

Judah was irretrievably doomed, Jeremiah concluded. There had been too much perversity for too many decades. Evil had become institutionalized, built into the entire system of society. Judah's persistent disregard for God's basic norms of justice and humility finally drove Jeremiah to pessimism. The situation was hopeless. Judah was as incapable of repentance as a leopard is of changing its spots (13:23). Catastrophe was inevitable, Jeremiah sighed. Ironically, he predicted, a nation even worse than Judah, would be the agent of God's judgment on Judah.

Jeremiah knew how his countrymen resented him. He had spurned their demands that he help support The Judah Way of Life. He felt despondent when they reminded him that it was un-Judean to criticize the nation. When he refused to attend the "I Love Judah" rallies, Jeremiah felt a deeper estrangement from his own people. He silently endured their pointed comments in his presence, such as "Judah—love it or leave it!" and "Back our King!" After hearing some of the superpatriots in the pulpits and street corners assure the populace that the national deity who blessed Jerusalem would protect Judah forever from the Babylonians, Jeremiah felt sick. The loneliness became almost unbearable. He felt dismayed at being called *traitor* and *subversive*. His deepest grief, however, came from knowing that his beloved Judah was rushing toward destruction in an insane, march-to-destiny convulsion.

Sometimes, the real patriot is the man accused of being disloyal. Sometimes a man loves his country so much that he will say *no!* when it insists on an irresponsible policy. In retrospect, we recall Niemoeller and Bonhoeffer as the German patriots during the Hitler era.

Young Jeremiah stood in his times as the most patriotic Judean, as in later times, the Man on the Cross came to be regarded as a very loyal Jew!

11
The Nonconformist

PROFESSOR GEORGE WALD made a well-known speech on the "Generation Without a Future," in which he pointed out that many of our young people today have a deep suspicion that they will not grow up because they fatalistically conclude that the bomb or war will end everything before they have a chance. In the film on Woodstock, the rock festival attracting 500,000 in the summer of 1969, the entire crowd stood to sing the chorus over and over, "We're all gonna die!" Hardly surprising that they are dubbed the *Now Generation. Now* is all they have to live in, when they feel that there is no future.

Daniel lived just after the midnight knell had sounded for his society, for his country, for his family, for him. War had obliterated everything. His nation was overrun by enemy troops. His beautiful home city had been reduced to smoking rubble. Relatives and friends lay dead or cooped up in stockades waiting deportation. It was the year 604 B.C., and the Babylonians had crushed Judah and destroyed its capital, Jerusalem. Doomsday had come for Daniel and his generation.

Worse, he was deported. As one of the young bluebloods of Judah, Daniel had been marked by the cruel conquerors for what everybody assumed would be a living death. Daniel and the flower of the nation were thrown like animals into the captive compounds, then pushed on a 600-mile forced march eastward across the Arabian desert to Babylon. Hundreds perished during the Bataan-like ordeal. Most of the survivors, often torn from families and companions, were scattered throughout the country of Babylonia, where many were eventually absorbed in the native population and lost their identity as Jews. Others were herded into camps for displaced persons.

The Babylonian emperor, Nebuchadrezzar, came up with a unique scheme. Possibly curious about the stubborn faith of the Hebrews he had such difficulty quelling, he decided to try an experiment in which he would try to Babylonize a few Hebrew boys.

Selecting four of the brightest youngsters from the best families of Jerusalem, Nebuchadrezzar gave instructions to his staff that the four boys were to be given a three-years-cram course in Babylonian culture. This intensive three-year Babylonizing program was intended to include total immersion in Babylonian literature, Babylonian language, Babylonian art, Babylonian customs—even the Babylonian diet and delicacies.

As many in the old days of the British Empire could testify, this same notion was successfully employed for promising young men in the colonies. A few years at Cambridge or Oxford would recast a boy from the jungles or bush into a model Englishman. Young Gandhi, from India, a product-victim of this system, described the way he found himself transformed into a dark-skinned miniature of the British ruling class, complete with accent, cane, and derby hat.

Young Daniel and three companions were selected by Nebuchadrezzar for the same kind of process. Strapping young Jerusalem aristocrats, they were educated to dress, talk, eat, drink, behave and think as Babylonians.

Even their names were changed. Daniel became *Belteshazzar.* His three friends were assigned the Babylonian names *Shadrach, Meshach,* and *Abednego.*

A name is a badge. When a person has his name taken away forcibly, he feels he is being stripped of part of his identity and deprived of a portion of his individuality.

In the spring of 1970, George Wrzyszcz, born in Scotland of

Polish parents, enlisted in the Gordon Highlanders and was unhappy when he became known officially in the British Army as
Pvt. XYZ because nobody could pronounce his name. "Maybe
they've changed my name," said George proudly, "but I haven't
changed it. I like the name Wrzyszcz."

Daniel and his companions were subjected to the demeaning
experience of being deprived of their Hebrew names. However,
Daniel continued to insist that he was still *Daniel*. The name Daniel
is Hebrew, meaning literally *God is my judge*. Although in a foreign country and under pressures to adopt a new life, Daniel determined to remember his heritage under God. His very name, a
vivid reminder of his faith as well as his family, was one he refused
to surrender. He resisted the Babylonians' subtle attempt to oblit-
erate his faith by assigning a substitute name.

The first open clash with the Babylonization program, however,
came over food. Nebuchadrezzar, anxious to introduce the four
young men to the Babylonian cuisine, left orders for his staff to
prepare and serve the youthful captives the rich delicacies of his
court. Knowing youthful appetites and knowing the sumptuous
fare of the royal kitchen, Nebuchadrezzar assumed that one of the
quickest ways to win over the four was through their stomachs.

As Hebrews, however, Daniel and his buddies had been raised
to observe the dietary or kosher laws. At the same time, their
mouths watered when the aromatic, tasty-looking meat dishes
were set before them. Furthermore, Daniel and his friends undoubtedly considered that they had to eat *something,* and, besides,
why draw the line over such a minor thing as food? Moreover, why
risk upsetting Nebuchadrezzar—especially over a silly trifle such
as what to eat?

Young Daniel preserved his identity in Babylon, remembering
his name, "God is my judge." Perhaps taking his cue from his
name, he persuaded his three fellow exiles to resist the pressures
to eat the illicit foods. Instead, Daniel asked Nebuchadrezzar's
staff for permission to eat simple vegetarian fare and drink plain
water for ten days, insisting that the four Hebrew boys would be
healthier-looking ". . . than all the youths who ate the king's rich
food . . ." (Daniel 1:15). Nebuchadrezzar's servants reluctantly

agreed to go along with Daniel's test, and after the ten days' trial period, were surprised to find that Daniel and his friends were more robust than anyone else.

At the end of the three-year Babylonization program, Nebuchadrezzar called for the four young captives. He noted with pleasure that Daniel and the others not only dressed and spoke like proper Babylonians but showed a decided superiority in ". . . every matter of wisdom and understanding . . ." (1:20). What Nebuchadrezzar could never comprehend, however, was that the clue to his four young protégés' wisdom and understanding lay in their faith. He thought that he saw four boys who had been cleverly brainwashed into being Babylonians, never suspecting that they knew that they belonged to God.

Daniel's faithfulness was not a flash of quick heroics. Rather, it was a steady, dogged day-in-and-day-out devotion to God. "And Daniel continued . . ." (1:21) the Biblical writer informs us, hinting that in spite of the way the Babylonian culture tried to grind down Daniel to its own shape, "Daniel continued . . ." to be *Daniel,* not Belteshazzar!

Daniel, like God's men in every age, was able to interpret the signs of the times. For example, while Daniel was still quite a young man, Nebuchadrezzar, the Babylonian emperor, was troubled with a frightening dream which he could never recall although it recurred so frequently that he turned into a pacing neurotic. Nebuchadrezzar called his troop of wisemen, soothsayers, advisers and experts in the occult, demanding that they not only interpret the dream but first describe the details of the dream. The emperor's staff obviously could not guess what his dream had been. Unable to help, the royal wisemen and soothsayers begged off. Nebuchadrezzar, however, angrily threatened them all with death unless they could tell him what his dream had been.

Daniel and his three friends prayed. Without any souped-up sensationalism, the Biblical account states that "then the mystery was revealed to Daniel in a vision in the night. Then Daniel blessed God . . ." (2:19). The point is not that Daniel worked some mumbo jumbo with the Lord for a special news flash; rather, in Daniel's own words, "No wise men, enchanters, magicians, or astrologers can show to the king the mystery which the king has asked, but there is a God in heaven who reveals mysteries, and He has made known to Nebuchadrezzar what will be in the latter days . . ." (2:27).

God the Creator and Sustainer and Redeemer of all men, Daniel boldly proclaimed, still discloses the ultimate purpose in the universe. This Almighty One proposes. He initiates. He empowers and directs. He effects. He intends to complete what He began. He holds His creation responsible for fulfilling His intentions. He judges all men, insisting that each is accountable to Him and to all others.

In an age which has seen an astonishing recrudescence of every form of ancient superstition, Daniel's announcement-*cum*-warning still stands. An estimated twenty million in the U.S.A. take astrology seriously. Graduate students in nuclear physics in prestigious universities write ecstatically about witchcraft. Books on black magic are best sellers on nearly every campus—and are seriously studied. Sorcery and spiritualism, Hare Krishna and voodoo, mind-expanding drugs and tarot cards have attracted more devoted disciples during the last two years than any major Christian denomination. From the Babylon of 2500 years ago in which Daniel lived to the Babylon of today, these primeval superstitions, dark and beastlike, have slunk back.

Daniel did not pretend that he could perform clairvoyant stunts or had any unique personal wisdom. As a put-down to all the magicians, enchanters, sorcerers and astrologers in Nebuchadrezzar's hire, Daniel's God gave Daniel insights into Nebuchadrezzar's disturbed thinking. Daniel accurately described the king's nightmare: a gigantic statue-image, with golden head, silver chest and arms, bronze hips and thighs, iron legs and clay feet towered in frightening majesty. Suddenly struck on the clay feet with a stone, the huge image crashed into speck-sized fragments which were carried away by the wind, while the stone grew to such size that it filled the earth.

Daniel then informed Nebuchadrezzar that the horrible dream meant that his world empire would collapse and be succeeded by three world empires before the final coming of God's Kingdom.

On another occasion, Nebuchadrezzar dreamed of an enormous tree which was chopped down by a being from heaven, leaving only a stump. Daniel, with his insights as a man of faith, interpreted the king's dream to mean that the monarch was going insane, and would grovel on the ground like an animal. Although Daniel pleaded, ". . . break off your sins by practicing righteousness, and your iniquities by showing mercy to the oppressed, that there may perhaps be a lengthening of your tranquillity" (4:27), Nebuchadrezzar haughtily ignored Daniel's counsel.

Nebuchadrezzar continued to strut and boast. Like Dame Edith Sitwell who commented only half in jest shortly before her death, "I know I ought not to dread death, but I am so conceited that I simply cannot imagine how the world would get on without me," Nebuchadrezzar proudly remarked one evening, "Is not this great Babylon, which I have built by my mighty power . . . for the glory of my majesty?" (4:30).

Daniel noted how Nebuchadrezzar studded his speech with *I, me, mine*. Discerning the egomaniac's habit of speaking so frequently in the first person singular, Daniel saw that Nebuchadrezzar had puffed himself into one who thought he could handle the Almighty. Daniel knew that when the king used such words as *power* and *glory* and *majesty* to describe himself instead the Supreme One, to whom alone such terms belong, Nebuchadrezzar was mocking God. Daniel held a view of history in which God will never be elbowed aside by any smirking tyrant. Therefore, Daniel knew for a certainty that a day of reckoning would eventually come for Nebuchadrezzar.

One year after Nebuchadrezzar recounted the tree dream to Daniel, Nebuchadrezzar went mad. Exactly as Daniel had predicted, the demented king foraged in the fields like an ox, eating grass, developing long clawlike finger nails and covered with a huge mat of unkempt hair.

Nebuchadrezzar's successor, King Belshazzar of Babylon, proved to be another swaggering, unstable dictator whose main interests were catering to his own caprices and entertaining his sycophants. One evening, during a lavish banquet, Belshazzar ordered the gold and silver goblets and trays captured from the Jerusalem

Temple brought in. In mock ritual, Belshazzar considered himself the life of the party by raising the sacred Temple ware and toasting and praising gods of gold, silver, bronze, iron, wood, and stone. To his horror, Belshazzar suddenly noticed strange configurations resembling lettering appearing on the wall. He stopped the feast, called for his magic-men and astrologers. In alarm, he stammered, ". . . Whoever reads this writing and shows me its interpretation shall be clothed with purple, have a chain of gold about his neck, and be the third ruler in the kingdom" (5:7).

Belshazzar's wise men dutifully trooped in, inspected the mysterious markings, and shrugged their shoulders helplessly. Belshazzar collapsed in a panic, rousing himself only when the queen had the presence of mind to call for Daniel who had answered perplexing questions during Nebuchadrezzar's reign. Belshazzar had heard of Daniel, but had been so busy being a playboy prince that he had never taken him seriously.

Daniel brushed aside all the king's offers of presents and spoke bluntly to Belshazzar. The young captive from Jerusalem told the most powerful ruler in the world at the time that Nebuchadrezzar had refused to acknowledge the sovereignty of the Most High God. "But when his heart was lifted up and his spirit was hardened so that he dealt proudly, he was deposed from his kingly throne and his glory taken from him" (5:20), Daniel continued, describing vividly the days when Nebuchadrezzar the lunatic ate grass like an ox. Turning to Belshazzar, Daniel told the startled monarch, "And you, his son, Belshazzar, have not humbled your heart, though you knew all this, but you have lifted up yourself against the Lord . . ." (5:22).

As for the markings on the palace wall, young Daniel grimly reported that they were a sign from God. The markings produced by a spectral hand, were the letters MN TQL PRS, according to Daniel. And the written message in those letters from the Lord at Belshazzar's feast, Daniel assured Belshazzar, should be read, *"He has numbered! He has weighed! He has divided! The Persians!"* Elaborating, Daniel pronounced total doom on Belshazzar. "This is the writing that was inscribed: MENE, MENE TEKEL, and PARSIN. This is the interpretation of the matter: MENE, God has numbered the days of your kingdom and brought it to an end; TEKEL, you have been weighed in the balances and found wanting; PERES [the plural of *parsin*], your kingdom is divided and given to the Medes and Persians" (5:25–28).

That same night, the Medes and Persians under Darius succeeded in taking over Babylon in a lightning-swift coup. Belshazzar was assassinated.

Daniel did not pretend to have some peculiar or occult powers. Humbly but directly, he asserted that his ability to discern the signs of the times was due to his conviction that "the Most High God rules the kingdom of men" (5:21). Any time that any man refused to live obediently before God and show compassion to other humans, Daniel stated, that man was flaunting God's rule and was in for serious trouble. "Practicing righteousness" and "showing mercy to the oppressed" (4:27) were two basic benchmarks of obeying God, according to Daniel.

We Christians today are the Daniels, the people who should be able to discern the signs of the times better than anyone else. No, we do not work ourselves into a spooky trance, nor do we vainly imagine that just being Christians makes us smarter than others. Rather, we look at all human events with a different perspective. Like Daniel, we know that everything that was and is and shall be is under the final purview of God. In our cases, we who have been radically affected by the Cross, Resurrection and coming of the Spirit carry the conviction that this God continues to be involved in history!

Signs of the times? Start with Daniel's benchmarks: "practicing righteousness" and "showing mercy to the oppressed." Look around carefully. Who are the oppressed today? Are they receiving mercy? Is that mercy specific? Is it enabling the oppressed to be freed and humanized?

It does not take any great perceptivity to observe if the oppressed are being helped. The Church today truly continues the Daniel-role when it interprets the times to the perplexed Babylon in which it lives.

Daniel, the Hebrew boy-captive, won recognition for his insights and wisdom. Under Darius, Daniel was appointed top man in the Empire. Nonconformist though he was, Daniel reached a position of immense influence and power.

Daniel also had his enemies. As a displaced person from a captured city, Daniel was sniffed at as a foreigner by some. Others resented his achievements and his blameless personal life. The sophisticates—the astrologers and sorcerers, enchanters and official advisers—never forgave him for excelling them on so many occasions. Darius' government, typical of every organization, had its rivalries and politics; a faction coalesced which schemed to push out Daniel from number one position. The only hitch, however, was that this faction could not frame Daniel on anything except his faith.

Knowing that Darius was a pushover for flattery, Daniel's enemies urged Darius to elevate himself as an incarnation of the Almighty and to forbid anyone from participating in any worship for thirty days except to venerate the king. King Darius, who, according to sculptures found by archaelogists, wore special elevator shoes to make himself taller than others, was easily duped into participating in the plot. Already secluded in an ornate palace, approachable only through intermediaries and surrounded by elaborate etiquette, Darius was delighted that his satraps wanted to deify him. He willingly agreed to Daniel's enemies further suggestion: a grisly punishment—the lion pit—for anyone caught breaking the king's edict during the thirty-day period.

The document was officially signed. Daniel's enemies rubbed their hands and waited to pounce.

Daniel, of course, knew that the document meant the death penalty for anyone caught in an act of worship apart from glorifying Darius. He could have played it safe and simply abstained from his daily prayers for a month. It would have been the simplest thing; he would not have caused a confrontation with either Darius, his boss, or the authorities. After all, Daniel was not compelled to worship the king, Darius. The edict did not affect any doctrine. No open apostasy was demanded. All that Daniel was required to do was to ease off on any open display of personal piety for thirty days.

"No need to be a fanatic or an extremist," Daniel could have told himself. "Besides, the law is the law."

And, he might have added, "Why take the risk? Better to forget your scruples and live to pray another day! Besides, how can I be so sure of God?" Daniel could have debated with himself.

"When I am in France," Napoleon declared during his Egyptian campaign, "I am a Christian; when in Egypt, a Muhammadan." This kind of casual commitment is what the world wants of disciples. Moreover, too often, it gets this kind of commitment. Research shows that most people—including church people—express different value hierarchies, depending upon what social role they are expected to follow at the moment. Like processionary caterpillars which play a lifelong game of follow-the-leader (and which, if the head of the first caterpillar is introduced to the tail of the last, will go round and round until the entire procession dies of starvation), most people—religious and non-religious—prefer to show conformity instead of commitment. It's more comfortable that way.

Daniel, a young nonconformist, refused to sell out his faith. At immense risk, he insisted on keeping his integrity by continuing his daily prayer sessions. In fact, he even continued to pray, as previously, before a open window facing his boyhood home, Jerusalem, knowing that he could be seen and reported. Daniel, aware of the risks, refused to compromise.

Daniel had no assurance that he would survive the lion pit. Come life or death, however, Daniel would not conform. Even if he were devoured by the lions and apparently received no vindication from God, Daniel stood fast. Whether God saved him or not, Daniel decided to remain faithful.

Daniel was arrested, convicted and dropped into a pit filled with ferocious lions threatening to devour him.

There are occasions when a man's faith means facing overpowering adversaries. On some of these occasions, the Christian knows that he could weasel away from expressing his commitment. And in a society where most would rather be called immoral than intolerant (a sign of our sickness, not our progress) it is easier to collaborate quietly with society's or Darius' dictates. Refusal to conform to current culture, whether in Darius' day or this day, may mean being pushed into a pit, where one will be forced to struggle with obscene beasts, such as despair, disgrace, temptation, fear, loneliness, defeat and death. Few Christians have the heroism to struggle in the pit with adversaries as wild and ferocious as these.

The Christian, however, knows also that God has already gone down into the pit. In the pit of the death and burial of Jesus Christ, God sacrificed everything for us. He knows our struggles with the roaring beasts. And at the Resurrection—God's final answer and final victory—God was victorious!

King Darius, who spent a sleepless night wondering what was happening to Daniel in the lion pit, hurried to the cave at daybreak, anxiously called, "Daniel, . . . has your God . . . been able to deliver you . . . ?" (6:20). Darius, knowing what usually happened when a victim was hurled to wild animals, did not expect an answer.

Daniel replied that his God, indeed, *had* been able to deliver him from the lion den.

The secret of Daniel's power lay outside the den. Although he has been alone with ferocious adversaries, Daniel was neither terrified nor torn apart.

Our God is able—able to deliver a Daniel from the den of lions, able to raise a dead Jesus from the pit of death.

God continues to act to deliver His people. No, there are no money-back guarantees insuring that every hour will be smooth and pleasant. Life will continue to have evil and mystery, brutality and hurt. God does not promise deliverance from problems and pain. The Able God, however, enables young men who feel like displaced persons always to be a generation with a future.

she had planned to marry. Would he take seriously the whispered rumors about her? Mary wondered. Would he conclude that she was a cheap tramp, a little slut who'd been sleeping around and got into trouble? Would he call off the marriage? Would he ever be able to completely believe her story? Would he think that her report about the mysterious Messenger from God was a cover-up for promiscuity? Mary felt like burying her head in her hands and weeping. The last thing in the world she wanted was to hurt the kindly and devout carpenter with whom she had planned to share the rest of her life.

What would she do? Where should she go, Mary asked herself. If Joseph turned her down, she knew that she would be branded as a whore or an adulteress. Would the irate, self-righteous villagers stone her to death? Or, would they drive her out of the area as a loathesome, wanton creature, condemned to drift to the brothels of Tyre or Damascus? And what would become of her Baby?

The Baby! "Throne of . . . David" . . . "reign over the house of Jacob" . . . "his kingdom" . . . "he will be called Holy" . . . "the Son of God" were the words used by the God-sent Intermediary to describe her baby.

Mary gasped. She knew well that each of these was a loaded word! A quiet, pious girl, she had sat each Sabbath for nearly all of her short life in the women's section of the Nazareth synagogue listening to the readings, and she understood perfectly that the words referred to the Messiah!

Mary, the plain peasant girl of Nazareth, betrothed to a fine but undistinguished craftsman in the village, was to be the mother of the long-promised Deliverer! She felt weak every time she thought about the idea. Within her body was to grow the life which, after being born, would develop into the Messiah of Israel! *She* would bring forth God's Anointed.

Why her? Mary was bewildered. Why did God choose her? Why not a rich Roman princess or a proud Oriental queen?

Waves of loneliness washed over her, as she tried to think through the meaning of the Announcement. A sensitive, devout spirit, Mary experienced the loneliness of one whose experiences or character are so different from others, the kind of loneliness her own Son eventually felt. She longed to talk with someone. But who would understand? Who would believe her story? She wanted to open her heart to someone sympathetic without being dubbed a freak.

Equally important, she wanted to get away from Nazareth. Then Mary remembered her cousin, Elizabeth.

Elizabeth was much older, and had become a sort of second mother to Mary. Married for many years to a priest named Zechariah, she had endured the disappointment and disgrace of being childless. Then, unexpectedly at an age when it was assumed that she was too old to have children, Elizabeth discovered that she was to become a mother.

Mary knew that in Elizabeth, she at last would encounter an understanding friend. Although Elizabeth lived some fifty miles to the south in the hill country of Judea, Mary left immediately. Of course, she had to walk the entire distance, traveling through some dangerous territory and over some rocky terrain. Exhausted and frightened, she burst in on Elizabeth.

Mary could not have picked a more understanding person than Elizabeth. Tears of relief spilled as Mary's story tumbled out. Mary received the strength and encouragement of Elizabeth's mature faith and wisdom. Day after day, they exchanged confidences. Mary was helped through the critical early months of her pregnancy. Most important, she caught Elizabeth's contagious sense of joy over anticipating a God-sent baby and learned to share Elizabeth's happy certainty in God's sometimes unknown but always correct ways.

Most of us, like Mary, sense that we are loners. Although we have many acquaintances, most of us have few friends. We all need Elizabeths, a person who will give time and understanding.

A certain psychiatrist in the midwest who is an alcoholic and a member of Alcoholics Anonymous needs an understanding friend. This distinguished psychiatrist looks up his butcher, who is also in AA, as the one understanding person whom he knows! It does not matter that the butcher has no clinical degrees or training; he *listens* and he *cares,* according to the psychiatrist, and that is what counts!

To the loners around us, especially bewildered young people, we can all be Elizabeths! More than sermons and programs, today's loners seek an understanding friend.

". . . My soul magnifies the Lord, and my spirit rejoices in God my Savior," Mary sang in a lovely prayer, "for He has regarded the low estate of his handmaiden . . ." (1:46–47). Buoyed by Elizabeth's support and friendship, the lonely girl prepared to return to Nazareth. Only Mary and Elizabeth shared the secret that Mary was the handmaiden of the Lord, but Mary knew that the entire village would soon know that she was going to have a baby. She braced herself for the barbs from the women at the market place. She readied herself for the coarse jokes about her which would be circulated behind the stables. Nazareth, with its earthy working-class peasant outlook, Mary knew, would aim its smirks and snickers, its censure and sarcasm at her. It would have been pleasant to have stayed in Judea with Elizabeth, Mary considered, but she resolutely made her way back home to Nazareth. She bravely decided that she would face Joseph and her fellow villagers.

Mary felt a resurgence of her former fright and loneliness as she wearily trudged up the path to Nazareth. The final mile seemed to be the longest stretch she had ever walked. Nobody, she knew, would greet her with the understanding of Elizabeth. There would only be the curious looks and awkward questions about her three-month absence. And soon, Mary sensed, her swollen body would reveal what most undoubtedly already suspected.

Her apprehension grew as she thought about her Joseph. She wondered what he had thought of her three-month unexplained sojourn in Judea. As she mulled over the sequence of events since the Messenger's visitation, Mary startled herself as she admitted that all the outward circumstances about her behavior pointed to something suspiciously like another case of an unmarried youngster running off after discovering that she was pregnant. And, remembering that Joseph was shrewdly perceptive, Mary felt herself sinking into another level of depression and loneliness; she reasoned that Joseph had already concluded the worst about her.

Mary quickly discovered that Joseph, indeed, had surmised that she was carrying a child. She tried to explain. Before the impassive carpenter, however, her words sounded hollow. She had hoped, even prayed, that Joseph would have some small degree of understanding. Mary, noting his stern expression, realized that her story sounded hopelessly implausible, and she faltered, then dissolved into tears. The lonely girl turned and left, hurt and dissappointed that Joseph could not understand.

Joseph, for his part, had no desire to make a public spectacle of his apparently unfaithful betrothed. According to the law at the time, he could have had her dragged into court. Instead, Joseph resolved to be as compassionate as he could under the circumstances. He prepared to initiate the necessary procedures to conclude the binding legal relationship of betrothal (in those times, betrothal—a step between engagement and marriage—legally bound the couple, although they did not yet live together). Joseph, many nodded, was an exceptionally just man to show such clemency. Ignoring the unsolicited comments of others who criticized him for not "teaching the girl a lesson," Joseph merely hoped that young Mary could somehow pick the broken shreds of existence and that he would be able to do the same.

Mary quickly received the report of the impending action. Trembling with fright and shame, she nonetheless steadfastly continued to trust God. She knew that nobody would receive her story of being chosen as the bearer of God's own Son, the Christ, and as she sat in her tiny peasant's hovel in dark isolation, she stubbornly continued to trust in the God who had surprised her with such staggering news.

Then Joseph appeared at her door. For a second, Mary sensed the elation of seeing her beloved again. Almost in the same second, however, she remembered the pain of his rebuff. What was he doing here, she wondered. Was this some fumbling gesture of a farewell? Had he decided to announce the separation plan in person? Had he stored up his anger and bitterness for so long that he finally had to come and vent it on her? Fearfully, Mary waited.

Hesitantly and slowly, the carpenter tried to talk. For a man who usually worked with tools rather than words, it was painfully difficult. Joseph's voice grew husky as he tried to express the impossible-to-express, namely, the conviction that God had plans for him and Mary together, and for Mary's unborn child. He meant for them to be married, Joseph stumblingly explained. It had taken something of a private revelation, according to Joseph, but he was certain that God intended for him to take Mary for his wife.

The girl was tempted to hesitate; she counted again the extent of her hurt over his refusal to have her earlier. It occurred to her that she could even the score by making Joseph squirm and wonder.

Did Mary consider turning him down, figuring that any man who could be so unfeeling once would be that way again, and therefore, not worthy of her? Did she lift her head in scorn, determined to wear her *panache* of personal dignity? Had she, in her loneliness, told herself that she would never lower herself again by offering to shed her self-respect? Was Mary thinking of being a proud loner, secure with her secret of being God's handmaiden and therefore, too good for any man?

Instead, this teen-aged girl who had already been subjected to deeper fears and loneliness than any woman ever, smiled and accepted Joseph. Mary agreed to commit her life and the welfare of the unborn Messiah she was carrying to the mercies of the near-penniless peasant-carpenter in front of her.

Mary sensed that there would be many, many difficult days ahead. Listening as Joseph gently told her, however, that they would name the baby *Jesus* (meaning *He will save*) Mary knew for a certainty that her trust in God was justified. And she trusted Joseph, and resolved to be his wife for as long as either was alive.

13
The Swinger

PUT HIM IN a well-tailored, three-piece suit and drop him into any American city or town, and he would have been a candidate for the Junior Chamber of Commerce "Young Man of the Year" Award. Still in his twenties, he would already have won all the badges of success: weekend cottage at the lake, with boat and too many free-loading guests; generous expense account, bonuses and stock options; country club membership; a sizable investment portfolio; paid-up mortgage; more-than-adequate insurance program; two cars; backyard pool; ten days on an island in the sun every Christmas; a week's skiing each March; company presidency in the offing; plans to retire at fifty. He would have known the System's rules, and followed them assiduously. And the System, clutching him to its bosom, would have rewarded him well, pampering him with prizes and conferring acclaim and respect.

He is young (the Greek suggests that he was between eighteen and twenty-four). He is well-off. He is successful. He is respected. He is the swinger who has everything.

Well, almost everything.

Secretly, this young winner is bored. And restless.

Do I want to go on like this for another thirty or forty years, merely making a good living but not doing much with my life? he muses. *I should be the happiest guy in the city, yet there is some-*

116

*thing missing. What do I do to find more meaning to everything?
Maybe this Jesus has some advice.*

The successful young man approaches Jesus. His air is faintly
patronizing; his question sounds like someone writing "Dear
Abby." He wants a couple of helpful hints such as can be found
in magazine articles with titles like "How I Can Find More Meaning In Life." Our successful young man expects Jesus to add a bit
of flavor to living. Heading the hospital drive and collecting pre-
Columbian art have not been all that enriching; perhaps Jesus
can give a practical suggestion or two.

". . . Teacher," the young man asks, "What good deed must I
do, to have eternal life?" (Matthew 19:16).

Jesus refuses, however, to pose as a quickie counselor. He will
not spoon out advice. Sizing up the questioner, Jesus moves beyond
the immediate question to the ultimate question. "Why do you ask
me about what is good? One there is who is good . . ." (19:17).
Jesus knows that the man's real questions or restlessness will be
not resolved until Mr. Success decides how he stands with God.
And for starters, how about the Commandments? Jesus asks.

The conversation has suddenly grown very sticky. This is not at
all the direction the well-to-do young man had intended the discussion to take. Accustomed to the deference that wealth brings,
the man had assumed that he would manage the talk with Jesus
just as he politely but firmly controlled his relationship with everyone else. As a man used to giving the orders, he is annoyed and
uncomfortable with the way Jesus has taken the initiative away
from him so slickly and put him on the defensive.

Our swinger agilely tries to steer the talk into a more general
and less personal track. Keeping the Commandments? Well,
Which? There now, he tells himself, *let this guru discourse harm-
lessly for a while on "religious values" or some similar topic. At
least I've headed him off from poking around in such personal
stuff.*

Jesus fakes out the man again. Instead of launching into a
windy discourse, Jesus crisply recites the last part of the familiar
list of Commandments every youngster learned as a child. It is
almost as if Jesus is saying, "All right; you want to play a little

boy's game with your questions, I'll give you little-boy answers!"

Luke's account of the interview adds the interesting detail that the well-to-do young man was a ruler, a synagogue leader, a respected and influential man in the local religious community. In this case, our man would have memorized and repeated the Ten Commandments countless times from his earliest childhood. He knew the A B C's of the faith as well as Jesus. Therefore, his question, *Which?*, was all the more a dodge, a bit of gamesmanship.

Jesus, ignoring the ploy, lists what the wealthy young synagogue leader had learned as a small boy.

What a list! Jesus presses the young man on his responsibilities before God on such basic matters as respect for the lives of others, his relations with women, his recognition of others' property, his respect for truth, his concern for his family. "You want some particulars about the Commandments," Jesus says in effect, "let's get down to cases. How about the Sixth, the Seventh, the Eighth, the Ninth, or the Fifth? What is your response to God's goodness in regard to these traditional clues?"

Jesus boldly sums up the second table of the Law (the second half of the list of Commandments) with the well-known verse from Leviticus 19:18: ". . . you shall love your neighbor as yourself . . ." A concern for others—this condenses the Commandments and answers the man's question, *"Which?"*

Astonishingly, the affluent, respected young churchman announces that he has lived up to the responsibilities Jesus outlines. ". . . All these I have observed; what do I still lack?" (19:20).

His reply shows that he has four hang-ups.

Hang-up number one: The swinging young religious leader thinks it is enough to be conventionally religious. He has observed the proprieties: he attends services (when he's not too tired to get up or isn't going surfing); he contributes (helps his tax situation); he sits on the official board (good for news releases and image building). He does the expected.

The moneyed young leader does not realize that with Jesus there is a big difference between being religious and responding to the love of God. He is unaware that ultimately religion is a form of self-worship, a type of idolatry.

Hang-up number two: The rich youngster is content with a righteousness based on negatives. He confidently tells Jesus all the wicked things that he has *not* done. He fancies himself exceptionally noble because of what he abstained from doing.

"I've never murdered anyone. I never ran around with other women," he chirps; "I never cheated or defrauded anyone. I never robbed."

It never occurred to him that with God, life must consist of more than negatives, but must include the positives of concern for a neighbor's welfare.

Hang-up number three: This man with the comfortable life style and comfortable faith style confidently assumes that he had kept all of the Commandments.

A silly notion! Actually, he—like everyone of us—had broken every one of the Ten in spirit or intent. The rich young leader blithely pretended to be an angel instead of admitting he was a sinner in need of help. Playing the phony before Jesus, he imagined that he was earning his own salvation by "keeping the Commandments."

Hang-up number four: This young man revels in comfort and security. He has devoted considerable energies in his young life in arranging his investments and property. He has no compunction about indulging himself.

After all, he asures himself, *It's mine, isn't it? I worked hard for it. And I can do what I want with it. Nobody's going to tell me how to use it, and nobody's going to take it away from me. Furthermore, anyone could have what I have if they work hard and learn how to swing the right deals.*

His little luxuries gradually came to be accepted as necessities. Besides, many of these could be written off as business expenses. His scheme of living has just as matter of course come to include a taste for vintage wines, custom-made suits, foreign racing cars and vacations in exotic places.

In spite of his hang-ups, this is a decent, pleasant young fellow.

And with his reputation and money, what a boost he could have given to Jesus' cause! Jesus' reputation, growing tarnished in the opinion of the Important People, could have been improved by signing up the rich young ruler. It would have been smart tactics by Jesus to have enlisted this respected, personable young man— at least as a tacit supporter, or maybe as a member of an ad hoc advisory committee if not as a full-fledged member of his disciples. After all, look at the hang-ups every other disciple had!

We moderns delight in trying to improve on Jesus. Like Monday-morning quarterbacks, we replay His strategy. Determined to have a comfortable, enjoyable religion, we soften and smooth His prickly demands. William Blake in a somewhat vulgar poem caricatured what many of us want.

> But if at the Church they would give us some Ale
> And a pleasant fire our souls to regale,
> We'd sing and we'd pray all the live-long day,
> Nor ever once wish from the Church to stray.
> Then the parson might preach & drink & sing,
> And we'd be as happy as birds in the spring.

Instead, Jesus confronts us rich, young rulers of every age and insists that we forget about security and comfort, and obey Him. His words jar and offend. ". . . If you would be perfect, go, sell what you possess and give it to the poor, and you will have treasure in heaven; and come, follow me" (19:21).

"How dare this Rabbi from Nazareth make such demands on me!" We bright, young-in-heart swingers (in secret, if not in fact) resent His words. We don't like ultimatums. Who does He think He is?

Therefore, we begin to argue irrelevancies, such as, "Suppose everyone gave everything away?" or, "Does this mean Jesus is encouraging give-away programs?"

The key point is that Jesus insists that the wealthy young swingers then and now take the risk of trusting Him. Jesus demands that we all rely on the miracle of God's acceptance.

In this particular case of the rich young leader in the interview,

Jesus dropped a non-negotiable demand: sacrificing his financial security by getting rid of everything he owned. Otherwise, Jesus knew, this individual had not the least possibility of knowing the eternal life he desperately sought.

For us who are well-off, successful, respected, and comfortable —the rich, young rulers of the 1970s—Jesus requires sacrifice equally as drastic. There is no painless, easy-credit discipleship. We who are so desperate to provide security for ourselves resent the claim that God alone is our certainty and safety. Stuck on our possessions, we bridle at any suggestion of sacrificing anything. The best most of us can muster is "organized charity, scrimped and iced, in the name of a cautious, statistical Christ."

For some, the sacrifice demanded of us may be to jettison opinions carefully cherished which have made us feel superior or secure. "I was brought up with the assumption that black people were inferior," one white woman confessed, "and for me the hardest thing as a Christian I ever had to do was give up all racist ideas, and folkways that had been drummed into me from the time I was a baby."

Jesus calls us to take the risk of trusting Him to sacrifice *whatever* we clutch to as our security blanket—a checkbook, prejudices, attitudes toward others, a cherished habit or hobby—*whatever!*

"Get involved," Jesus orders the successful young swinger. "Get involved with others!"

The rich young ruler is safe, so secure, so shielded, never feels others' pain, never cries with them. And Jesus knows that such a creature is not completely human. Jesus, aware of the desperate need for the wealthy one to be touched with love, expressed His care and interest. At the same time, Jesus indicated that the young aristocrat would have to show some response to God's concern by touching others with love.

"Get involved with others," Jesus insisted, "particularly those who are hurting and needy. Get involved with the needs of the poor."

For those of us who are relatively well-off and successful, the poor today are the non-white members of our population.

To be black in America is almost certainly to be poor. The majority of black Americans are poor. The poorest Americans are black, and even the most prosperous blacks are still poorer than great numbers of whites. The unemployment rate among black married men is twice that of whites. Three out of ten working-age black men are out of a job or earn too little. Most black people earn less than their white counterparts.

Four out of ten black American children are officially classified as poor, living in families in which the incomes are below the minimum for health and decency to sustain life. Two-thirds of those children are not receiving any aid. Sociologist Dr. Kenneth Clark has likened what happens to black youngsters in the ghetto "to the dehumanization which occurred in the Nazi concentration camps," concluding that our apathy toward the poor is causing the same scars on the souls of children as those on the survivors of Dachau, Auschwitz or Buchenwald.

Because these persons are poor, they suffer. Four times as many black mothers die in childbirth as white mothers. Three times as many black babies die in infancy as white babies. The average life expectancy in the United States for a black person is sixty-one compared to sixty-eight years for a white.

A nation that spends $75 billion on defense and one-tenth of that to help the poor, or $17 billion on tobacco and liquor, ten times what is spent on the war on poverty, has not shown the will or intention to be involved with the poor.

The person who speaks only of his rights, prates about his property values, and clamors for sterner repression of black unrest misses encountering the Christ of the Gospels. Although he may clothe his stance and efforts in Biblical verbiage, he is concocting a fictional Saviour, a Mary-Poppins Jesus. Any talk about the Lord without a profound concern for and deep involvement in the needs of the poor is cheap folk religion and romantic fantasy!

Jesus summoned the rich young ruler to contribute to his neighbor's good. To know eternal life, Jesus instructed him to respond to the divine goodness by showing a positive concern for those who were hurting. Jesus will not permit him—nor anyone—the luxury of watching from the sidelines or of thinking only of saving his own soul. The risk of trust means an involvement with the poor.

At the time Jesus met the young swinger, the Master was on his way to Jerusalem—and the cross. When Jesus said, "Follow me!" he commanded the man of means to share a life of radical obedience and sacrifice. Jerusalem was the riskiest place for Jesus or any of his followers to go.

"If you are prepared to make unheard-of sacrifices and to engage in drastic forms of involvement," the God-Man states, "then my young friend, you are invited to come and follow me—to Jerusalem—and a crucifixion and resurrection."

A century ago, San Francisco newspapers carried advertisements for Pony Express riders. WANTED: YOUNG SKINNY WIRY FELLOWS NOT OVER EIGHTEEN. MUST BE WILLING TO RISK DEATH DAILY. ORPHANS PREFERRED. APPLY CENTRAL OVERLAND EXPRESS, ALTA BLDG. MONTGOMERY ST.

This is roughly what Jesus demands of all rich young rulers. A cross, not a cushion, still stands as the symbol of our faith. Following Him to a personal Calvary is the necessary prerequisite to resurrection.

14
The Militants

MOST OF US remember our childhood Sunday school materials. Invariably, the illustrations portrayed Jesus' followers as weary old men in immaculately clean silk gowns. Elderly and enfeebled, desiccated and delicate, the disciples resembled a group of geriatric cases. Unfortunately, we continue to carry mental pictures of Jesus' men as frail septuagenarians, squeezed dry of emotion and ambition.

In actuality some of Jesus' Twelve should be labelled *militants!* Two of these, in fact, were dubbed *Sons of Thunder* by Jesus.

The two Sons of Thunder were a pair of fishermen-brothers named James and John. Like the tumultous storms which unexpectedly broke over the Sea of Galilee, sudden, angry moods rushed through these two. They bristled with the same arrogance and intensity as today's militants.

Nothing blah or bland about James and John! As aggressive and tough as their nickname implied, they worked hard, laughed hard and cursed hard. All their lives had been spent in boats and out in the elements. With powerful shoulders and outsized hands, the two brothers were used to handling any difficulties with a primeval simplicity.

One day, for example, they ran across a healer who claimed

124

that he was casting out demons in the name of Jesus. John glowered. He had never seen this healer anywhere near Jesus.

Pushing his way through the crowd, John took a menacing pose in front of the man. "Are you part of Jesus' disciple band?" the Son of Thunder demanded. When the startled healer admitted that he was not, John sternly told him to quit healing in Jesus' name.

Hearing the healer starting to protest, John's face clouded like an ominous thunderhead and his eyes flashed like summer lightning. Censoriously, John repeated his command to stop healing in Jesus' name.

Nervously, the man glanced at John's powerful fists. The healer stopped using Jesus' name in his exorcisms.

The next time the Sons of Thunder saw the Master, they self-righteously announced that they had encountered some stranger healing in Jesus' name, but John had really put down this interloper. James and John felt immensely self-important. Intolerant of anyone not sharing their vocabulary, they talked as if they owned the copyright on Jesus' name. And they acted as if they had a monopoly on Jesus' power!

Jesus, of course, set these two militant disciples straight in a hurry, reminding them that they had no special rights or privileges. Jesus made it clear to James and John that they were not the good guys, with all others second best. Furthermore, Jesus told them that they were not necessarily the only ones who could heal in His name.

". . . we forbade him because he was not following us" (Mark 9:38) John thundered darkly in reply.

Jesus rejected such narrow partisanship. He rebuked the rebuker. Such officiousness as John's reflected petty jealously and a desire to guard his own importance.

". . . Do not forbid him [the healer]," Jesus continued, "for no one who does a mighty work in my name will be able soon after to speak evil of me. For he that is not against us is for us" (9:39, 40).

Jesus' next words to His stormy disciples indicated the militant type of caring with which He meant for all men to comfort others. "For truly, I say to you, whoever gives you a cup of water to drink because you bear the name of Christ, will by no means lose his reward" (9:41).

Jesus does not care who gets the credit, so long as His loving life style is exhibited. When He finds His own people insensitive to those in need, He surprises us by conducting His ministry through unlikely people. When He notices that His followers are unwilling to reach out in compassion, He shames us by working through unorthodox methods.

For example, when the Church became so preoccupied with its wealth and prestige in southern France in the twelfth century, He raised up an underground church group called the *Cathari* ("the pure") who lived in poverty and preached self-denial. Or, in fourteenth century England, when the institutional Church forbade the Scriptures to be read in English, He motivated roving groups of Bible-quoting preachers known as the Lollards.

With wild and wonderful disregard for ecclesiastical neatness and niceties, the Holy Spirit often introduces the bubbly, explosive new wine of the Gospel into strange and exotic bottles. Who knows? Are non-institutional forms such as folk-preaching, jazz masses, the charismatic movement and Christian communes the Cathari and Lollards of the 1970s? Before anyone rebukes anyone else participating in a street ministry or healing service "because he was not following us," a rereading of the Master's message to His militant institutionalists, James and John, is in order!

In spite of the militancy of James and John, Jesus appreciated their enthusiasm and commitment. Better a fervid, burning sense of concern than a casual, lukewarn response. Before we over-thirty types write off the young, militant churchmen who disturb us with their unsettling tactics on behalf of peace and/or justice, we need to recall that at least two of the Twelve showed similar traits and tendencies. Nevertheless, Jesus called them and patiently worked with them.

In fact, He not only chose them as part of the Twelve, but initiated them and Peter into an inner circle. The trio of names, Peter, James, and John, constantly reoccurs in the Gospel accounts. These three militants (and Peter fits the description, too!) were specially selected to accompany Jesus on some of His most difficult calls, such as the time Peter's mother-in-law had a severe fever, or Jairus' little girl lay dead. The Sons of Thunder and Peter as Jesus' closest intimates climbed the slopes of Mt. Hermon with Jesus and experienced the startling breakthrough of Jesus' divine identity known as the Transfiguration. The same three militants were asked to sit up with the Lord as He prayed in Gethsemane. The militants among the disciples occupied a special place in Jesus' heart and work.

True, Jesus had to channel their militancy. He worked to temper their belligerency. It was not always easy. Their blustery temperment sometimes blocked the purposes of Jesus' Kingdom. On some occasions, Jesus seemed to have failed altogether to harness the thundering drive of James and John.

There was the time, for instance, when Jesus and his disciple crew were proceeding toward Jerusalem for Jesus' final visit. One evening, Jesus sent messengers into a Samaritan village requesting hospitality for his Twelve and Himself. Word came back that the villagers contemptuously refused. This was an unspeakable breach of common courtesy in that area at that time.

When James and John heard how rude and inhuman the Samaritan villagers had been, they exploded, ". . . Lord, do you want us to bid fire come down . . . and consume them?" (Luke 9:54)

Here were the original confrontation activists! Hot-tempered and indignant, James and John strained to unleash their totalitarian impulses. Kill for the love of Jesus; destroy the vindictive Samaritans; return cruelty for cruelty!

When God sends down fire, however, it is for rebirth, not for ruin. He *loves* us into line. Hate for hate, spite for spite is never the way of the One who was known as the Builder, never as the Destroyer. "I came that they might have life," He insisted, "and have it abundantly" (John 10:10).

For any who impetuously jump to call down fire on those opposing God's rule, Jesus still sternly turns and rebukes. Jesus refused to accede to his militant young follower's ultimatum.

Nonetheless, knowing that when one harnesses a torrent, one has power, Jesus kept the stormy Sons of Thunder as part of the Twelve's inner circle.

Like all militants, Jesus' two Sons of Thunder at times seemed to have been fueled with raw ambition. They desired privileged places and preferential treatment. Knowing that Jesus claimed to be the long-promised Messiah-Deliverer, James and John approached Him one day and asked a favor.

". . . Grant us to sit, one at your right hand, and one at your left, in your glory," they demanded (Mark 10:37), assuming that they had an incontestable claim to Jesus's ranks. Backing them was their mother, who thought that nothing was too good for her boys.

The irony of this selfish request for preeminence is that it came immediately after Jesus' second announcement of His coming suffering and sacrifice for others. James and John, however, had obviously missed the point. Assuming that Jesus' Kingdom was a grab for earthly power, these two greedily schemed to secure the positions of honor for themselves. The Sons of Thunder grinned in anticipation, thinking of the trappings of a typical Oriental court, with fawning lackeys and an elaborate pecking order. The inner circle surrounding every kinglet or caliph received honorific titles and obsequious deference. Glory Boys James and John boldly bid for the powers and perogatives of the number two and three places in Jesus' coming kingdom.

". . . You do not know what you are asking . . ." Jesus coldly replied (10:38). He noted their jealousy and pride, their blindness to His real mission. King He was, but not with the usual trappings and mannerisms. His rule came through service, not swagger.

Few of us are true Jesus people. Even those of us claiming to be closest to the Christ secretly assume that we deserve a few perquisites. Knowing how insidiously present this thinking is even to Christian preachers, a group of missionaries interned in Japan during World War II had the practice that the man whose turn came for preaching the sermon for Sunday worship also found that it was his turn to clean the toilets that morning. John Coventry

Smith, who was there in the internment camp, recalled, "Getting down on your hands and knees to mop the floor and wipe the urinals keeps one humble enough to preach the gospel an hour later . . . I should recommend to all preachers our Sunday morning preparation."

Ambitious for preferment, James and John wanted not to serve but to be served.

". . . Are you able to drink the cup that I drink, or to be baptized with the baptism with which I am baptized?" Jesus asked (Mark 10:38). The *cup* (as in Isaiah 51:17, 22) meant voluntarily accepting *suffering.* The "baptism" (as in Psalm 42:7, Psalm 69:2, Isaiah 43:2 and Luke 12:50) meant the initiation into *martyrdom.* Jesus knew that He would be called upon to lay down his very life. He must have felt like crying or cursing over the obstinancy and obtuseness of James and John. Three years' private discussions about His rule coming through sacrificing for others, and all these two could babble about was what they could get for themselves! If these, two of the three of the inner circle, had such shallow understanding of His ministry, how could anyone understand his *cup* and *baptism?* With such flimsy followers, how could God's rule ever be brought to pass?

Cup? Baptism? Sure, why not? ". . . We are able" (Mark 10:39) James and John, the militants, glibly answered.

When the others in the disciple band overheard the discussion, they ". . . began to be indignant at James and John" (10:41). Like squabbling, petulant children, each disciple resented the way James and John were trying to claw their way to the best seats. Who did they think they were? Besides, why shouldn't it be I? After all, *I* am just as good as either of those two hotheads. Why shouldn't *I* get something out of following Him?

For men and women of every age who are militantly ambitious to get something for associating with the Master, Jesus has jarring words. Perhaps the big shot ideal pervades the thinking of every group or association throughout society. "But it shall not be so among you;" He sternly warns. ". . . whoever would be great among you must be your servant, and whoever would be first among you must be slave of all" (10:43–44). And the Greek word for servant or slave means flunky or lackey of the toilet-cleaning type, not liveried staff member with managerial responsibilities!

James and John felt their mouths drop open at Jesus' choice of words to describe what it meant to be part of His group. Servant? Slave? This ran completely contrary to everything they had ever known!

Underlining these remarks with a reference to His own life, Jesus added, "For the Son of man also came not to be served but to serve, and to give his life as a ransom for many" (10:45). A few days later on Golgotha, Jesus acted out these words to the last syllable.

At a small chapel on the famed Duomo Square in Florence, Italy, there is an inconspicuous side door on which the words appear MISERICORDIA FRATERNITY. The Misericordia Brotherhood was founded in Florence in 1246, by a group of Florentine aristocrats who discovered during a terrible plague (which wiped out a third of the population) that to be a Christian is to be a slave of others. Donning black robes and masks to make them anonymous, these aristocrats worked as stretcher bearers among the helpless and poor.

The brotherhood still continues its serving, providing most of the ambulance service and much of the welfare work in Tuscany. Today, men of all classes belong to the Misericordia Brotherhood, from laborers to nobility, each serving at least one hour a week, shaving a bedfast old man, bathing an invalid, or performing other personal service. The ancient tradition of anonymity continues, however, so that the emphasis is on serving without thought of personal acclaim. For over seven hundred years, the Misericordia Brotherhood has observed the practice of thanking those they have helped, crossing their arms, bowing, and saying to those they have just served, "Thank you for needing me!"

A person with such a selfless spirit of service has swung into line in the happy parade of the Jesus people. A militant refusal to think of one's own advancement and a militant insistence to care for the needs of others is the type of ambition which those who march behind Jesus are meant to have.

Jesus calls ambitious, militant people—people with the kind of ambition and militancy which makes them aspire to be cheerful fellow sufferers with Him. The Master's militancy means a cross, laying down one's life for others.

James and John, the Sons of Thunder, eventually grasped this hard-to-learn type of suffering love. Blasted by the confrontation of care on the Cross and Resurrection from their selfish posture of radicalism, James and John were precipitated into the exhilarating adventure of radical selflessness.

About A.D. 42 to 44, Herod Agrippa was advised to quash the obnoxious heretics claiming that Jesus was the living Messiah. Execute the most prominent, he was urged, and make a public example out of this individual to cow the others. Whom to seize and kill? Naturally, the most outspoken young militant for the cause of Jesus. And who was that person? James, of course.

James was the first of the Twelve to die for Jesus. James was the only one of the disciples whose marytrdom is mentioned in the New Testament (Acts 12:2).

Although James was beheaded, John refused to be scared into silence. He boldly continued Christ's ministry, preaching the Good News of the Kingdom and demonstrating it through acts of healing and mercy.

Those who are militantly Christ's, however, do not cringe before Herod's hooded headsmen. James and John, for example, the old Sons of Thunder, actually "died" some time about the time of the first Easter, and were transformed into new personalities, James and John, *Sons of Wonder!* Such men sit easy in the saddle of life and death. They smile. They know that God's militant act of love on the Cross conquers all!

15
The Revolutionary

IN A RECENT experiment, readers were shown mock copies of *TV Guide* and asked to pick programs they thought they would like to watch. In each copy, three fictitious programs were listed: "Two Scientists," "Freedom Fighters" and "Innocent Man." However, each copy showed a different sponsor for the make-believe programs. The sponsors were Alcoa, GE and something called the National Protestant Church. When readers made their selection of preferred programs, which one came in last? Each time, it was the one sponsored by the National Protestant Church, indicating again that most people assume that anything connected with the Church will be dull and insipid.

It was not always that way. Look at the original Twelve. Whatever you may call these men, you cannot label them dull or insipid. Take, for example, the man identified as Simon the Cananean by Matthew and Mark, and Simon the Zealot by Luke.

Simon the Zealot carried an ugly, curved dagger concealed under his cloak. Because this dagger was called a *sica,* Simon and his Zealots were sometimes called *Sicarii.* Simon, trained to stab to kill with one sudden, vicious lunge, had taken a solemn oath to use his *sica* against anyone committing any sacrilegious act or stirring up any anti-Jewish feelings.

Whether called Simon the Zealot or the Cananean, the idea was the same: be the agent of the jealous God to exact vengeance on transgressors. *Zealot,* in fact, comes from the word meaning *jealous.* *Cananean* (*Kanna'im* in Hebrew) derives from *El Kanna,* the term for a *jealous God,* as in Exodus 20:5.

The *Kanna'im* or Cananeans boasted that they had the right to kill on sight any non-Jew caught inside the sacred precincts of the Temple in Jerusalem. An inscription from the Jerusalem Temple found in 1871 specifies that the death penalty was automatic for any Gentile passing beyond that point, and Simon the Cananean prided himself that he had the honor of guarding the sanctity of the Temple and the Law.

Simon, a ferocious fanatic, gloried in his membership in the Zealots. His favorite folk heroes were Simeon and Levi (two of Jacob's sons who avenged the family honor after their sister Dinah was raped by Shechem by slaughtering him and his followers), and Phinehas (who took his spear and cleaved a Hebrew man cavorting with a Midianite girl, preventing the pollution of the tribe and the spread of plague). Simon listened eagerly to the stories idealizing these men as models of good Zealots.

More than anyone, however, Simon and his fellow Zealots honored Mattathias the Maccabean as the prototype Zealot. About 164 B.C., Mattathias, a doughty priest, angrily killed both a fellow Jew who was sacrificing to heathenish deities and a royal Seleucid officer on duty to enforce the edict. Forced to flee, Mattathias and his sons ignited a revolt, refusing to pay taxes, raiding Seleucid garrisons, and organizing a resistance movement passionately devoted to freedom. (The valiant Maccabean freedom struggle is recalled by our Jewish neighbors each year in the Feast of Chanukkah which falls near our Christmas celebration.) One such band of fighters at the time of the Maccabees called itself the Zealots. Simon's cohorts liked to think that their movement stemmed from Mattathias' revolt.

Simon's Zealots or Cananeans came into prominence as an organized entity, however, during Herod the Great's reign a few years before Simon was born. Angered by the way Herod had forced Romanizing practices and building programs on Jerusalem including a Roman gymnasium, Roman arena, Roman bath, and

Roman trophies (images to which homage was to be given), and
determined to punish Herod's many crimes of bloodshed and idolatry, a group of ten men plotted to kill him. The ten assassins hid
themselves in the theater where Herod was supposed to enter.
Herod's efficient secret police, however, tipped him off, and he escaped. The ten were caught and tortured slowly until they died.
Later, however, a civil disturbance broke out, during which the
crowds literally tore to pieces the spy who leaked the plan to the
police. The ten plotters were celebrated as popular hero-martyrs.

Near the end of his reign, Herod installed a huge golden eagle
over the Great Gate of the Temple. Judea's populace again seethed
with indignation. Two leading rabbis mobilized forty young men
to tear down the hated eagle one night in a bold raid. All were
caught and cruelly burned to death on Herod's personal orders.

The resistance movement began to flourish. In Simon's father's
day, ardent patriots banded together, determined to put an end to
Herod's brutal tyranny. In Simon's home area of Galilee, Sepphoris—about five miles away from Nazareth—became the main
hotbed for revolution. Many families suspected by Herod's ubiqui-
tous agents were forced to flee. Living as outlaws, hiding in caves
and ravines in Galilee with their wives and children, these fierce
fighters formed the nucleus of what became the political party,
the Zealots.

Simon as a youngster heard the stirring reports from older men
of heroic episodes which took place in places Simon knew well as
a boy. Not far from Simon's home, for example, was the cave
where one Zealot had made his personal stand against Herod's
troops. Willing to fight to the death for his convictions and for
freedom, this stalwart rallied his seven sons, shouting defiantly,
"Let us die rather than transgress the commands of the Lord of
Lords, the God of our fathers. For if we do this, our blood will be
avenged before the Lord." Simon also heard the report of another
Zealot in his locality who, when discovered by Herod's police,
killed his own wife and children rather than permit them to be
taken as slaves by Herod.

Simon, however, not only listened to stories of such heroics
during his impressionable years, he also witnessed them. Although

Simon could not personally remember the time of Herod's death, he knew how the pent-up resentment exploded and he saw the results as a small boy. Desperate nationalists, led by Judas the Galilean tried to overthrow the Herodian dynasty. The first century historian, Josephus, a turncoat Jew, reported, "The nation was infected with their [the Zealots'] doctrine to an incredible degree, which became the cause of its many misfortunes, the robberies, and the murders committed." Simon grew up in the midst of this violence.

In A.D. 6 when Simon was still a small child, Judas the Galilean and his Zealots rebelled when the Roman governor, Quirinius, tried to conduct a census. Judas, according to Josephus, "taught that God is the only Ruler and Lord, and neither death nor any dread should make them call any man Lord." Fired with Judas' oratory, the fanatic Zealots swarmed into Sepphoris, captured the Roman garrison, seized the arms, and sparked an uprising against Rome. Simon had childhood recollections of fervid, armed men moving stealthily through his village as the revolt spilled throughout Galilee.

The Romans under Varus cruelly crushed Judas and his forces. Sepphoris was burned to the ground, and all of its inhabitants were sold into slavery. Later, two thousand men—among them, two of Judas the Galilean's own sons—were publicly crucified. Young Jesus must have watched from the hilltop of Nazareth. Young Simon knew all about it, too. Both boys had an early acquaintanceship with crosses, and carried no false illusions about a crucifixion.

Judas the Galilean left a fraternity of fiercely dedicated Zealots. Judas' remaining son, Menahem, called for continued resistance to the Roman enslavement. Forced to go underground for a time, the Zealots hardened into a secret para-military outfit of super-Jews who insisted on avenging any affront to the Law or the nation. More and more, however, the Zealots began to emphasize political nationalism. Some Zealots refused to look at or handle a coin bearing Caesar's image, insisting that this was tantamount to knuckling under to Rome. Others would not enter a city where statues had been erected by the gate. Others pledged to kill any

Gentile who listened to any discourse on the Law unless he under-
went circumcision. Relentless and uncompromising, the Zealots insisted that they would bring in the kingdom of heaven by force.
God's rule would come, the Zealots promised, when the despised
Romans were expelled. To drive out the Romans, the Zealots reasoned, would take violence. Since violence was necessary, the
Zealots trained themselves to destroy with grim efficiency.

Young Simon was nurtured on the glorified atrocity stories of
the Zealots by the old-timers in his home village. He heard the tone
of admiration and pride in the voices of the older boys as their
big brothers slipped off to join Judas the Galilean. Simon sensed
the rage and resentment among the Galileans when Varus tried to
stamp out the rebellion with such harsh methods. Although we
have no way of knowing, Simon probably lost members of his own
family in the fighting or in the rows of the crucified. Such a high
proportion of the best of young Galilean manhood had perished
that a heavy residue of anti-Roman feeling remained. Young Simon, caught in the slipstream of hate, nationalism and gory piety,
bought his own *sica* and joined the movement.

The clandestine meetings, the constant danger, the midnight
raids brought a certain exhilaration to Simon. At last, he was really
doing something! The Zealots, he convinced himself, had the answer. Topple the System, drive out the Romans, and a new order
could be created. The Zealot way, Simon agreed, was the most
viable form of action. The direct immediacy of slashing or burning
had an appeal. A *sica* thrust or a blazing torch got results!

Such a misplaced idealist as Simon would have felt quite comfortable with his modern fanatic counterparts such as the Al
Fatah, the IRA, the Weathermen, or the post-Marxian branch of
the SDS. Hand Simon the Zealot a grenade or firebomb, and he
would have been one more in the ranks of those driven to irrational violence to gain their objective.

A person who turns to violence so constantly and so viciously
gradually becomes emotionally unbalanced. Perhaps due at least
in part to the violence in our culture, ten million young people
under twenty-five currently require mental health treatment in the
U.S. today (and only 500,000 actually receive any attention).

Although only about 1 percent of the present college generation
are SDS types, already espousing violent overthrow of present society, another 12 to 15 percent are radicalized enough that they
would take up violence if forced on them. Reliance upon destruction and cruelty indicate problems in the person as well as the
system. Perhaps unwittingly speaking for many flirting with revolution "for the hell of it," one bright twenty-year-old senior spoke
feelingly of "the need to get my head together."

Simon's *sica* was destroying his psyche. Overkill began to make
him subhuman. Claiming to be jealous for God, Simon became
zealous for gore.

Through the years of Simon's early manhood the Zealots
stepped up their terrorism. Their acts became more irrational as
they aimed their raids not only against the Romans but against
fellow countrymen not cooperating with Zealot leaders. The Romans, in turn, tried to crack down. Reprisals led to counter-
reprisals. Barbaric cruelties by oppressor caused a ferocious and
reckless brutality by the oppressed. At times, in Galilee the Roman
procurators faced near-anarchy, and even the Pharisees criticized
the Zealots for their senseless slaughter and wanton excesses, calling those in the resistance movement *heretic Galileans.*

How did such a young man as Simon the Zealot ever get hooked
up with Jesus Christ? Where did they meet? What did Simon find
in Jesus? What induced Simon to desert the Zealots to join Jesus'
movement?

The Bible gives few clues, stating simply that Simon the Zealot
(or the Cananean) was among those chosen by Jesus to be one of
the Twelve. Obviously, Simon and Jesus became closely associated
at some point early in Jesus' ministry. Apparently, the two young
men from Galilee found such a degree of mutual trust between
them that Jesus deliberately selected the one-time Zealot to be one
of his most intimate associates.

Jesus is described as *Saviour,* bringing *salvation.* Both Saviour
and salvation came from the New Testament word *sōtēr* which
means *health* or *wholeness.*

Simon the Zealot realized his need to get his head together.
Pulled apart by irrationality and rage, Simon turned to Jesus for

healing and wholeness. He sensed that the savagery of the *sica* was driving him insane.

Any relationship with Jesus Christ means being with the One whose personality is a unifying force. This means wholeness—being put together again. Disintegrating personalities are firmed and patiently rebuilt, which is merely pyschological jargon for *salvation,* church shorthand for the same experience.

Undoubtedly, Simon the ex-Zealot also recognized that Jesus Christ embodied The Way, The Truth, and The Life, making pale the ways, truths, and living of the underground. In Jesus Christ, Simon found both revolution and revelation.

However dull and insipid some modern churchmen may appear, do not ever apply these adjectives to Jesus Christ! Any personality who could attract such a dedicated and ruthless man as Simon the Cananean can never be labelled *dull.* Any individual who could command the loyalty of such a fanatic revolutionary as Simon the Zealot can never be called *insipid.*

Simon, who traded a revolution through a *sica* for revolution through salvation, quickly found himself in unusual company. One of the Twelve with whom he had to associate was Matthew, a former tax collector and collaborator with the Romans.

In their careers prior to knowing Jesus Christ, each man had been pledged to destroy the other. Simon had solemnly vowed to kill on sight anyone cooperating with the Romans, particularly despised tax collectors. Matthew, as one who had sold out to the Romans, would have furnished the procurator with names and addresses of any known Zealots.

Astonishingly, here were two men who once would have done everything possible to have the other killed! Within the same group of the Twelve were two sworn enemies—two committed to murder each other!

What kept Simon from plunging his *sica* into Matthew's belly when they were first introduced? What prevented Matthew from slipping away to leave a note with the nearest Roman patrol to have Simon the Zealot arrested?

The only explanation, of course, lies in the power of Jesus' personality. Resurrected from killers by the creative care of God exhibited in the Christ, Simon the one-time Zealot and Matthew the former tax collector took new vows, promising to pass on Life to each other.

Simon the Zealot and Matthew the tax collector in Jesus' band of disciples reminds us again of the nature of the Church. The Twelve, with all their disparity of backgrounds, were working models of the new community brought into being by Jesus Christ. In spite of their differences, both Simon and Matthew were called to be part of Christ's family. Each was needed; each was valued. Each had been received as one of God's closest relatives by Jesus; each turned toward the other as brothers.

Simon and Matthew and the others were a miniature of every one of our congregations today. We gather with little in common. There are sharp differences—in outlook, goals, background, culture, and needs. Recent events have made those differences more real. And our differences rub raw sores on each other. Almost without exception, we are polarized into suspicious factions in every congregation. Criticism has given way to denunciation, and denunciation now threatens to give way to excommunication, at least in thought and intention; or, if we cannot push out the others, we threaten to walk out ourselves.

Jesus Christ, who brought us all together, keeps together as His Church. He will not let us break away from each other. In spite of our differences (and they are considerable, as in the cases of Simon the Zealot and Matthew), He who is still the Head of His family, the Church, *means for us to be together!*

There are few references to young Simon, the onetime Zealot, in the New Testament. In addition to mention of his name in the list of the Twelve in Matthew, Mark and Luke, the only other occasion where Simon's name comes up occurs in Acts 1:13, where Simon is on the roll of those in the Upper Room after Jesus' crucifixion.

What thoughts went through Simon's head at the time of the crucifixion? Did all the old anti-Roman hatred surge back? Was he tempted to sharpen his *sica,* hide it under his cloak and resume the old way?

Some of his old cronies in the Zealots undoubtedly told him,

"C'mon back, Simon. Rejoin the real revolutionaries—that guy you were following—look what happened to him! Done in by the Romans, the same as any sucker or weakling gets done in by them. Come with us, Simon. We'll show you where it's really *at*. Get in on the action! The Zealots don't namby-pamby around. Our *sicaes* talk for us! We get things done, like fast, man. And we're the only ones who're going to change things."

Grabbed and held tight by the revolutionary love revealed in the Leader who died with a prayer of forgiveness for the violent men who executed him, Simon stood fast. The former Zealot had seen many, many crucifixions, but never a crucified One like this.

Simon the Zealot, the young extremist resistance fighter, found Jesus Christ led the biggest, greatest, longest-lasting and farthest-reaching revolution. Traditions have been passed down that Simon the Zealot faithfully promoted the Gospel, organizing revolutionary cells of Christian believers throughout Armenia before dying a martyr's death.

Compared to Jesus Christ, all other revolutionaries and movements are dull and insipid. Zealous, daring men willing to risk everything for change discover that He is still the most dynamic, creative and powerful revolutionary ever.

16
The Cop-Out

HIS ADULT NAME, Mark, means *large hammer*. As a boy, however, he seemed to have all the hard striking power of a cream puff. Actually, *Mark* was his Greek name, and came later; *John* (meaning *God is gracious*) was his original Jewish name. In the Greek-speaking first century world (where Jewish men often adopted Greek names), John, the Jerusalem Jewish lad, eventually became best remembered as Mark the Evangelist.

Although his father died while Mark was still young, Mark enjoyed upper-middle-class comforts. He and his mother lived in a large commodious house, complete with private gate to the street and a large room on the upper floor which accommodated many guests. They even had servants, making young Mark somewhat soft and pampered.

Typical of many adolescents growing up in the home of a devout parent, young John Mark took his faith for granted. He wore the label of Church member, but was a casual rather than a committed believer. Mark descended from a well-known family of Jewish Levites, some of whom had settled on Cyprus. He drifted along in the ancestral faith, proud of being born a Hebrew of the Hebrews but content with a second-hand religion.

When his mother, Mary, affiliated with those associated with a Galilean rabbi named Jesus, young Mark made a few gestures

141

toward being part of the small group. He even went through the embarrassment of carrying a water pitcher one day on the street to help the cause. Mark protested at first because carrying pitchers was woman's work, and no self-respecting boy wanted to be caught in public with a water jug on his head. He finally agreed to bear the silly pitcher, however, when it was pointed out that this would be the only way Jesus' group would be able to identify a person who could lead them safely to Mark's mother's house. Mark grumbled, but served as guide for the disciples who prepared the Last Supper in the Upper Room.

To Mark, however, the group upstairs at first was just another gathering of guests from Jesus' group. He peeked through the doorway to satisfy his curiosity. As he listened as Jesus and his Twelve talked and ate, Mark became intrigued. He wanted to stay outside the door and eavesdrop. When Mary insisted that he get ready for bed, Mark reluctantly undressed and wrapped himself in his linen sleep-robe.

There was much getting ready to happen, Mark sensed. He could not have gone to sleep that night if he had tried. He had heard the rumors circulating through the city about Jesus. Mark knew that a crisis had built up between Jesus and the authorities. There had been reports that the authorities had secret plans to arrest and execute Jesus before Passover.

As he lay awake, Mark heard the sounds of a man's footsteps going down the steps. He thought that this was so strange that it hinted at something ominous. No one ever left a Passover meal. Why had one of the Twelve left? Mark wondered. The only reason anyone ever broke the fellowship of a Passover meal would be to break off a relationship, Mark considered. Did this mean, he asked himself, that one of the disciples had defected?

Mark listened intently. For considerable time, he could hear the low sound of Jesus talking. Much later, he heard the group upstairs sing a hymn followed by the unmistakable noises signifying that the party had broken up and that everyone was leaving. Instantly alert, Mark jumped up and slipped out of the house after the group. He noted that Jesus had only eleven with him. Where, the boy wondered, was the twelfth?

Mark trailed behind the band as it made its way through the darkened streets out of the city to the olive orchard called Gethsemane. Hiding behind a tree in the shadows, he overheard Jesus ask for some of his group to join him and pray. Everyone, Mark observed, seemed exhausted. Mark watched Jesus walk to one side, sink to the ground, and begin to pray audibly. Surprised at how quickly the others dropped off to sleep, the boy saw Jesus come back several times to his snoring companions, pleading with them to keep him company.

Suddenly Mark caught sight of the flickering torches and the glistening weapons which seemed to move in from all directions. Heavily-armed police had them surrounded, Mark noted. He saw one man walk up to Jesus and give him the familiar embrace of a pupil to a rabbi and the lad recognized the man as one who had been in the Upper Room for the Passover. A moment later, Mark grasped that this one had turned traitor, and was embracing the Master as a signal to identify Jesus to the police. Mark decided it was time to get out of there. As he heard shouts and the clanging of swords being drawn, the boy started to run.

Suddenly, Mark felt powerful hands grabbing him in the darkness. The guards had him! He twisted. He felt the guards seizing his nightshirt. Jerking to one side, he broke free, leaving the ripped garment in the hands of the swearing trooper. The naked boy ran as fast as he could through the dark orchard, slipped across the brook Kidron, and raced through the streets until he reached his home.

Too frightened to venture out during the next few days, Mark did not see the ghastly sight of Jesus' crucifixion; however, he heard the reports. A few days later, he also heard that Jesus had been raised from the dead. Mark wondered.

His mothers' house became the headquarters of those in Jerusalem who found themselves waiting to see what they should do after Jesus' resurrection. Mark looked in on the group from time to time, but did not make a great effort to involve himself with the followers of Jesus. He noticed several weeks later that after a large number had been praying in the room upstairs, everyone seemed fired by the Presence of the Holy Spirit. Mark admired their en-

thusiasm and courage. Remembering the way the soldiers had tried
to seize him that night in Gethsemane, however, he did not allow
himself to take many risks for the news of Jesus.

He enjoyed the excitement and the comings and goings at his
mother's house. He never forgot the night that Peter somehow
broke out of jail during Herod's persecution of the Jesus people.
Mark remembered how their servant girl, Rhoda, had been so
stunned at seeing Peter at the gate that she screamed and rushed
inside to tell everybody in the house, leaving poor Peter still
pounding desperately to get in! Mark teased Rhoda for days about
that.

One year while Mark was still a teen-ager, a crop failure, a food
shortage and rising prices struck the Jerusalem area. By that time,
the Church had spread throughout the Middle East. Conscious of
the want and hardships among many Christians in Jerusalem, believers in more affluent congregations sent a special famine relief
offering to the Jerusalem Church. This special fund was entrusted
to Barnabas and Paul, two leaders in the Antioch Church to the
north in Syria.

When Barnabas and Paul arrived in Jerusalem, they naturally
stayed with Barnabas' relatives, John Mark and his mother. Barnabas and Paul needed help in administering the fund, and turned
to young Mark.

Mark proved to be a valuable aide during the famine crisis. He
enjoyed the responsibility and took statisfaction from doing something to help others. He delighted in the excitement of serving.
Typical of many young people, however, Mark sometimes showed
an impulsiveness and immaturity. His faith at that point was a
blend of altruism and enthusiasm. He could not articulate the
meaning of the Gospel well. Although he affirmed a commitment
to Jesus Christ, his response spurted and sputtered. One moment,
Mark's Christian discipleship soared, the next, it sank. While handling relief supplies for needy church families, Mark's zeal winged;
soon after, it wheezed.

Mark liked working with two such strong, masculine personalities as Barnabas and Paul. He had been too much of a momma's

boy for too many years. It was reassuring to Mark to be accepted as a man by men.

When the time came for Barnabas and Paul to return to Antioch, young John Mark begged to be allowed to tag along. Barnabas and Paul, who enjoyed the youngster's company and appreciated his enthusiasm, knew that they could always use an extra pair of hands in the programs for the Gospel. Furthermore, the two older men saw immense possibilities for mature service for Christ within young Mark, and wanted to encourage this potential to develop.

Later, prompted by the Holy Spirit, the congregation at Antioch took the momentous step of commissioning Barnabas and Paul as pioneering missionaries. Barnabas and Paul were packing, preparing for a long journey, when Mark asked to accompany them. The two men discussed it briefly, and gave their permission.

Mark was elated. Although he had not been officially set apart by the Antioch church for the missionary journey the same way Barnabas and Paul had, Mark prided himself on being a full-fledged member of the team.

His title was assistant or attendant to Barnabas and Paul, but Mark felt flattered by the way the two older men treated him as a sort of junior evangelist and not as a mere flunky. Mark cheerfully carried their bags and ran their errands, but he also helped teach and catechize.

For Mark, it was a lark. Crossing from the coast of Syria by ship to the east coast of the island of Cyprus, the trio gradually made its way from Salamis across the lovely island to Paphos on the west side. It was April, just after the opening of the navigation season. The climate was delightful. The people—many of them Mark's relatives—showed a warm hospitality. The missionaries received a cordial hearing and enlisted many followers. At Paphos, for example, they succeeded in winning the local Roman magistrate —the first non-Jew converted by Paul—to the cause. The two-month tour of Cyprus could not have been more pleasant or rewarding.

At Paphos, on the western edge of Cyprus, Barnabas and Paul

decided to take a ship to the Pamphylian area on the coast of what
is now southern Turkey. Mark, who had assumed that the group
would retrace its steps and return to Antioch, had misgivings about
continuing. When the three missionaries disembarked at the port
of Attalia, a steamy furnace in midsummer, Mark wished that he
had not come.

The little party hurried inland to Perga. Hemmed in by the
5,000 to 9,000 foot Taurus ridge, shut off from any cooling winds
and heated by the relentless Mediterranean sun, Perga and the area
of Pamphylia has one of the most enervating climates in the world.
Marlaria and fevers, until recently, were endemic. Paul, who
gradually had been emerging as the leader of the group, displacing
Barnabas, came down with a debilitating illness—his *thorn* as he
called it. ". . . you know," Paul later wrote the Galatians, the inhabitants of the area to the north where he and Barnabas founded
a string of tiny congregations, "it was because of bodily ailment
that I preached the gospel to you at first . . ." (Galatians 4:13).
Because of Paul's illness, the decision was made to push on immediately to the interior.

The interior! What foreboding that brought to young John
Mark! For one thing, there was the journey itself—a hazardous,
exhausting climb over the rugged Taurus mountain range. The
area had the reputation of being infested with bandits, mostly
runaway slaves who usually killed first and robbed later. In some
places, the trail clung to the side of steep cliffs overlooking dizzying drops of hundreds of feet below; in other places, it led to the
banks of dangerous, icy mountain torrents, which had to be forded.
Travelers dreaded the trip up and over the Taurus. Mark knew
that he would not have just a one-way journey but a round trip
through the wild Taurus mountain country, and two such trips
seemed to be stretching one's luck. It frightened the youngster.

The romance of traveling with Barnabas, his cousin, and Paul
was wearing thin. Sweltering in Pamphylia and climbing the Taurus was a far cry from rambling through sunny Cyprus with its
smiling people and balmy breezes.

Why had they bothered to leave Cyprus, Mark wondered. Why
didn't they stay where the people were "our own type"? Why

bother with these strange-speaking outsiders, with their hostile looks and peculiar customs. Besides, there was plenty of missionary work where they'd come from, and missions should start at home, Mark told himself.

And whose idea had it been to land in this humid, inhospitable place? Paul's, of course. Mark was growing irked at the way Paul had turned into the one giving the orders instead of cousin Barnabas. In the book of Acts, in the narrative of the beginning of the first missionary journey, Barnabas' name is listed ahead of Paul's. From Pamphylia on, however, it is always "Paul and Barnabas." Mark, immature and jealous of his cousin, was not a big enough spirit to permit the more-able Paul to assume the leadership. Furthermore, Mark felt uneasy about Paul's increased tendencies to preach to Gentiles. Paul was growing too liberal for Mark's tastes. To a boy with a devout Jewish upbringing, Mark thought that Paul's willingess to preach the Gospel to non-Jews was disturbing. What would the folks back in Jerusalem say?

Jerusalem seemed to be farther and farther away. Away from home for a long time and for the first time, John Mark disliked the thought of traveling to a still more remote area and remaining away from home for an indefinitely long period. This was not in the original bargain, Mark told himself. Besides, he had his mother to consider. Who was looking after her? What if another famine had hit? Young Mark remembered that it had been months since he had had any word from home.

Scared, homesick, and annoyed at Paul, Mark convinced himself that he did not have to continue. He had signed on for a trip to Antioch, and then a quick jaunt through Cyprus, he reasoned within himself. When he remembered the ship in the harbor heading for the coast of Judea, John Mark made up his mind to drop out of the missionary party.

There is a persistent report dating back as early as the third century that Mark carried the sobriquet, *the stump-fingered* or *mutilated in the fingers*. Does this title infer that Mark had some deformity? Could it imply, as some suggest, that perhaps Mark had a malformation of the toes and was partially lame? Or, as others insist, could the epithet, *stump-fingered* be a synonym for a ma-

lingerer in the army, meaning that Mark got the reputation for
being a deserter?

As far as Paul was concerned, the title, *deserter,* fitted young
Mark. Paul tried to urge the wavering youngster to remain. When
Mark insisted on dropping out, Paul felt wounded. Part of the hurt
came from the fact that Mark was the cousin of the man who was
Paul's best friend at that time. There was an ironic twist to having
a desertion by a cousin of Barnabas, the man who had been Paul's
supporter when nobody else had stood by Paul—Paul's help in
time of need on two occasions. Mark's dropping out reflected on
the Gospel Paul lived for. It also hurt Paul's efforts. Paul surmised
that many would say, "What kind of fly-by-night cause is this?
Even its believers cannot agree or stay together."

Determined to drop out, Mark paid for his passage and packed
his belongings. He could not look Paul or Barnabas in the eye
when he prepared to leave.

Mark disembarked at Caesarea and hurried home to Jerusalem.
He quickly noticed that many in the Jerusalem Church also had
deep misgivings about bringing non-Jews in the Christian fellowship. Mark reported what he had seen Paul doing. To his immense
satisfaction, he discovered that most shared his opinions about
Paul and about Gentiles.

Mark, enjoying the limelight, found himself invited to speak to
groups of tradition-minded Christians who insisted on holding on
to all their Jewish practices. Mark's detailed accounts of Paul's
welcoming noncircumcised outsiders to the faith upset many.

When Paul and Barnabas returned after enduring incredible
hardships and opposition while planting a string of tiny Christian
cell groups in Galatia, they encountered a chilly reception. Mark's
reports had made the Jerusalem believers and many others ex-
tremely uneasy about Paul.

A Church Council was called to discuss the matter of inviting
non-Jews into the Church. Mark listened to Paul as he presented
his case, and grudgingly agreed with the rest to admit Gentiles into
the faith without being circumcised.

Shortly afterward, Mark accompanied Peter as an assistant
when Peter and a few others traveled north to Antioch to talk further with Paul and Barnabas. Mark, embarrassed and guilty be-

cause of the way he had dropped out of Paul's group in Asia Minor, felt defensive. Although it made him uncomfortable, he went along with the others to the common meals in which former Jews and former Gentiles ate together.

Mark was relieved when some of the ultratraditionalists who would not dine with uncircumcised arrived from Jerusalem. Mark knew that they would set things straight. It reassured Mark to hear the reactionaries talk so convincingly. In fact, Mark noted with pleasure, even Peter and Barnabas reverted to their old Jewish life style, separating themselves at meals so they would not have to eat with noncircumcised Christians.

Paul was disgusted and disappointed that such men as Barnabas and Peter had allowed themselves to be intimidated by the super-conservatives. Paul told Peter to his face that he had regressed back to Legalism by refusing to eat with non-Jews, and had abandoned the Gospel.

Mark, immaturely thinking that his prime loyalty lay with a faction, deeply resented Paul's criticism of Peter. By implication, Mark also understood Paul to be indicting Barnabas. As far as Mark was concerned, any criticism of his cousin Barnabas—especially by Paul—was an affront to Mark himself. The touchy youngster imagined that Paul had insulted the family honor. Hearing Paul refer to Peter and Barnabas being carried away by the "circumcision party" (Galatians 2:12) Mark thought in terms of *we* versus *them*. The headstrong youth, stinging under rebuke toward Peter and Barnabas, told himself, "If this radical Paul accuses my friend Peter and my cousin Barnabas of being swayed by the reactionaries, he puts me in the same category, because I am with them." Trying to assert his *machismo,* Mark nursed his bruised pride—and betrayed his youthful immaturity.

When Paul and Barnabas got ready to team up for another missionary trip, relations were strained. Paul grew indignant when Barnabas announced that Mark would accompany them again. Paul pointed out that Mark had dropped out from the work on the previous journey.

During World War II, a man who did not measure up to the high standards of a Commando was let go, returned to the unit from which he had volunteered. There was no punishment, no al-

ternative, no argument. The ultimate shame was RTU—RETURNED
TO UNIT.

Paul with his steely sense of discipline and commitment, dismissed Mark as an RTU. "I cannot take the risk of taking along a
deserter, a quitter," Paul growled.

Barnabas, whose name literally means *Son of Encouragement,*
replied, "I cannot abandon a kid who has good stuff in him and who
shows promise of developing into a strong leader."

Each, of course, was correct—to a point. However, neither
would yield. Hot words followed. After the angry exchange over
Mark, the two one-time friends and coworkers separated. Paul
teamed up with Silas and left for Asia Minor. Barnabas took his
young cousin, Mark, and sailed for Cyprus.

Mark smarted under the rebuff from Paul. He knew that he had
hurt Paul, but he told himself that Paul had also hurt him. Mark
found himself fueling his hurt by recalling all the unpleasant little
personality traits Paul had—all the occasions in which Paul had
irritated him. He bristled with animosity toward Paul and festered
with resentments. If he never saw Paul again, the boy assured himself, it would be fine.

Mark, however, recalled what had happened between God and
man through the crucified-resurrected Jesus Christ. He knew that
in Jesus, God had sought out the unlovable to bring about new
relationship. God's reconciliation with him, he remembered, could
become real only when Mark would be reconciled to Paul. Until
he greeted Paul as a brother, his faith was a sham. Inspiring
preaching and heroic deeds would be affectation until he asked
for Paul's forgiveness, the boy grasped.

Mark finally suffered the hardest of all deaths—the demise of
proud dignity. He sustained the personal crucifixion of self. The
cop-out asked Paul for forgiveness—and realized the resurrection
experience of receiving forgiveness!

P. T. Forsyth, the English theologian who had personally
plumbed the depths of the meaning of the Cross and Resurrection,
described the forgiveness encounter for every one-time cop-out:
"I was changed from a disciple to a believer, and transformed
from being a lover of love to being an object of grace!"

17
The Failure

TIMOTHY often felt like a failure. The son of a Greek-Gentile father and a Jewish mother, Eunice, the boy did not feel that he belonged in either community. Although exposed to the robust faith of Judaism by his devout mother and grandmother, Timothy never acquired the hearty toughness of those saturated in the Law and the prophets. Timothy, in fact, had not even been circumcised as a boy—at first perhaps out of deference to his non-Jewish father, perhaps because of squeamishness on the part of the womenfolk later on.

The boy was raised by his mother and grandmother. Although he deeply appreciated their care, he sometimes pressed for more freedom. Timothy had no father in his home during many of his formative years, and, denied a relationship with a positive, masculine figure, sometimes contemplated his sense of failure. Other boys were robust; Timothy was shy, sensitive and sickly. Timothy carried deep feelings of inferiority and inadequacy.

One day, a visitor arrived in Timothy's home town of Lystra. This visitor's arrival hit the town like an air raid. The name of this visitor: Paul, the Christian Apostle. Never had anyone in Lystra, particularly young Timothy, ever encountered any personality like Paul.

Timothy with the other boys followed the strangers, Paul and his companion Barnabas, to the center of the town. To everyone's amazement, Paul and Barnabas healed a lifelong cripple. Timothy watched eagerly as the delighted townsfolk acclaimed the two visitors as reincarnations of the gods Zeus and Hermes.

Timothy noticed, however, that the two strangers refused to accept the accolades. Timothy listened as the leader of the two, Paul, set the record straight in a hard-hitting address. Perplexed at the references to someone called Jesus the Messiah, Timothy wondered what these two men were up to.

Timothy's fellow townspeople at Lystra, however, were incensed. Feeling that they had been duped by the strangers and somehow cheated of a visit by the gods, the townsfolk grew ugly. Some of the ringleaders began to heckle the two who called themselves Christians. When the two Christians boldly stood their ground, the crowd changed into a mob, and push turned to shove.

Young Timothy looked on with horror. Throughout the rest of his life, he never forgot the scene. Amidst the dust and roar, he saw the two Christians brutally beaten. The townsfolk had changed into raging animals, Timothy noted. He could not believe that people he knew could be so insanely angry and cruel. For a few moments, Timothy thought that he should do something to try to stop the mob, or try to do something to help the two strange men who called themselves Christians. But what could he do? Timothy asked himself. And he felt the pangs of failure again because he could not do anything constructive.

Timothy, wide-eyed with fright, watched the mob, like an enormous, mindless beast with deep murderous roars, carry the two Christians like prey to the dump at the edge of town, then disgorge the victims. The two men did not move, Timothy observed, but lay like crumpled bundles of rags and hair where they had been thrown. Timothy considered going up to them to see if he could do anything for them. When they continued to appear lifeless, and when the townspeople glowered menacingly, young Timothy decided not to go too close, at least for the present. For a moment he struggled again with his failure-feelings.

That night, long after dark, Timothy heard noises at the door. Opening it, he was amazed to see the two terribly-mauled strangers who had been left for dead that afternoon. Speechless with fear, excitement, and wonder, Timothy motioned the men inside and brought his mother and grandmother, Eunice and Lois. He listened as the two bleeding men whispered that they had come because they had heard that Eunice and Lois, God-fearing Jews, would aid them.

As the two women dressed the wounds and fed the badly injured Christians, Timothy watched and listened eagerly. He heard the spokesman, Paul, describe his journeys on behalf of the most amazing Personality ever to live, Jesus, the long-promised Messiah, God's Chosen. Timothy wondered. How could any Personality move two men like these followers to go through such ordeals so willingly and so cheerfully? This was not the first time that they had been beaten, he learned. What a tremendously exciting and significant kind of living these two, Paul and Barnabas, had, Timothy thought. Compared to his own timid existence, these Christians had a direction and a drive! With a renewed sense of inadequacy Timothy regretted that he had always been so reluctant and wishy-washy.

At the same time, he was fascinated by the reports of Jesus Christ. The news that Paul and Barnabas described meant that through this Jesus, God came to make contact with people who were failures, among others. This meant, Timothy thought with joy, that God sought out him, the timid boy of Lystra! The news seemed impossible. Yet, as the boy intently listened to Paul's conversations the rest of that night, he became convinced that it was true! He felt elated. This was the greatest news that he had ever heard! In Jesus Christ, he was certain, God accepted the little, lonely failure named Timothy!

Paul and Barnabas, cleaned up and refreshed, limped away from Lystra before daybreak. Timothy, however, could not forget them.

When Paul returned to Lystra a couple of years later, Timothy was overjoyed. He and his mother, Eunice and grandmother, Lois, took the momentous step of associating themselves as part of the Christian nucleus in Lystra.

Timothy, a bashful youngster, had never known as vital a person as Paul. In the hero-worship phase of his development at the time, Timothy made the gnarled old Apostle his idol. The delicate, diffident boy adopted Paul as a sort of father figure.

Paul, who had no family of his own, was deeply touched and began to call Timothy "my beloved and faithful child in the Lord . . ." (1 Corinthians 4:17). Furthermore, Paul noted Timothy ". . . was well spoken of by the brethren at Lystra and Iconium [a neighboring town]" (Acts 16:2). Remembering how he needed assistance on his missionary tour, Paul asked young Timothy to accompany him as part of the missionary staff.

Timothy's mother, Eunice, had grave reservations. For one thing, she was reluctant to see her only son (who was the family breadwinner by this time) leave home. Furthermore, Eunice knew the dangers which Paul—a marked man in most cities—and his staff faced. Eunice, however, overcame her instincts to overprotect her boy and let him go.

Timothy himself had misgivings about accompanying Paul. He still carried vivid memories of the scene when Paul and Barnabas had been left mangled, bloodied, near-corpses outside of town after preaching Jesus Christ. Although Timothy considered himself a disciple (Acts 16:1), he shrank from rough stuff. He quavered when he thought what might lie in store; nonetheless, he marched off from his hometown with Paul.

Before the little party left, however, the congregation at Lystra gathered prayerfully to lay hands on Timothy in an ordination service. It was a solemn moment. Timothy acknowledged his commission, promising those present that he would do his best to be obedient to Christ in carrying out His ministry. In the years that followed when the going grew hard, Paul occasionally bolstered Timothy's faltering faith by gently reminding him of that memorable service in Lystra. "Fight the good fight . . . take hold of the eternal life to which you were called when you made the good confession in the presence of many witnesses," the grizzled old warrior-Apostle wrote (1 Timothy 6:12), admonishing Timothy on another occasion to ". . . be steady, endure suffering, do the work of an evangelist, fulfill your ministry" (2 Timothy 4:5).

Finally, before leaving, Paul did an apparently puzzling thing by insisting that Timothy be circumcised. Paul previously had denounced the rite as worthless, had criticized the Christians in Galatia for clinging to the practice as necessary for salvation.

Timothy was puzzled. Going through circumcision seemed so inconsistent with all that Paul had taught him. Had Paul not told him that a Christian was free from legalism and ceremonial? Timothy remembered Paul's emphasizing that a person is saved by what Jesus Christ does, not by superstitiously following rules. "Why," Timothy wondered, "should I observe the minutiae of the Jewish code in this way? Is this not trying to manage my own salvation? Is this not the very thing that I *don't* have to do?"

Timothy, however, learned that there were occasions where he would have to learn to sacrifice his personal convictions for the sake of the consciences of others. Specifically, Timothy learned that at that time and in that place, it would be impossible to open dialogue with pious Jews so long as he remained uncircumcised.

Timothy remembered that he had been commissioned to accompany Paul as a Christian evangelist. If they were going to get a hearing in the Jewish communities of the Roman world, Timothy agreed that he would have to avoid offending the sensibilities of their listeners.

Timothy, the young missionary, agreed to submit himself to the obsolete and unnecessary. He voluntarily gave up the liberty he proclaimed, forsook the freedom he could have claimed.

Luther neatly stated the meaning of this paradox. "A Christian man," he wrote, "is the most free lord of all, and subject to none. A Christian is the most dutiful servant of all, and subject to everyone." (*Treatise on Christian Liberty.*)

Paul and Timothy understood that a Christian *is* a perfectly free lord, subject to none, but will, out of concern for others on occasion, forget his freedom and rights. The theses of freedom and slavery under Christ seem contradictory to those in the kindergarten stage of the faith. Wise old Paul from the graduate school level of discipleship correctly grasped that there is a place for both freedom and servanthood. "For though I am free from all men," he wrote, "I have made myself a slave to all, that I might win the more" (1 Corinthians 9:19).

The point still stands. For example, Christians know that they are free to drink or not to drink. There are no rules and one's salvation does not depend upon being a teetotaler. However, many voluntarily give up their freedom to drink out of concern for the nine million adult Americans who are alcoholics, and the hosts of crippled personalities who are tempted to rely on the glass crutch. These abstaining Christians dare not pretend that their abstinence is a salvation-by-works ploy. Knowing that there are no strictures against enjoying God's creation, they are not blue-nosed ascetics. These Christians, perfectly free to drink and subject to no rules, are trying to be dutiful servants of all in order that no other be tempted or weakened.

Commissioned and circumcised, Timothy joined Paul's party as it pushed westward. The group, after several aborted attempts to evangelize in western Asia Minor, was led to take the momentous step of crossing into Europe. Timothy, part of the missionary team which helped plant the Church in the western world, found himself in Macedonia in what is now northern Greece.

He also found himself in grave danger. In Philippi, the first stop in Europe, Paul's sizzling preaching landed Paul and Silas in jail, chained in stocks after receiving a horribly painful beating. Although Timothy escaped the beating and arrest, he was terrified. Fragile Timothy remembered vividly the scene a few years earlier in his hometown on Paul's first visit. Realizing that he was under surveillance as a member of the missionary party, Timothy felt so queasy from fear that he could hardly eat.

When the earthquake destroyed the Philippi jail, miraculously freeing Paul and Silas, and permitting the entire party to get out of town, Timothy felt better. He half-hoped that Paul would decide to call it quits.

Instead, Timothy found his stomach tightening into a painful knot when he heard Paul announce that they would push on to the next city, Thessalonica, and try to plant a Christian congregation there.

Thessalonica was like a rerun of the scene at Philippi. Timothy, quivering with fright, watched Paul endure another severe mauling. The tensions began to take their toll on the boy. Timothy's nerves started to give him health problems, causing Paul to pass on home-spun medical advice such as ". . . use a little wine for the sake of your stomach and your frequent ailments" (1 Timothy 5:23).

The little missionary band fled southward through Greece, stopping at Berea, where it was decided to split the group. To get Paul to safety, some disciples whisked him south by sea to Athens. Timothy and Silas stayed on at Berea for a time to bolster the newly-organized church, then rejoined Paul, who by that time had settled at Corinth. When word reached the group that the struggling congregation at Thessalonica was experiencing difficulties, Timothy was sent as Paul's emissary to investigate and encourage. Timothy discharged his minor duties, returning with the good news that the new converts were staying true to the faith. Timothy, Silas, and Paul jointly wrote two letters to the Thessalonian Christians to reinforce their commitment.

Shortly after writing the second letter to the Thessalonians, Timothy, Paul, and Silas moved from Corinth. The Corinthian congregation, however, continued to be a problem church. About A.D. 57 Timothy was sent back to Corinth as Paul's troubleshooter.

Timothy felt elated. At last, he had been entrusted with a real assignment! This was his first big responsibility. And he was on his own! Here was his opportunity to prove himself to Paul, to the others, and to himself. Timothy, who had always previously been nagged by a sense of inadequacy, jubilantly marched into Corinth to take over for Paul. Corinth, Timothy assured himself, would be the turning point in his personal career. He, too, would win his spurs!

Typical of congregations then as well as today, the Christians at Corinth had allowed the contemporary culture to flavor their life style. In fact, the Corinthians in the Church were hardly distinguishable from those not in it. Worship services had degenerated into mayhem as everyone tried to speak at once. At the common meal in which the Lord's Supper or Eucharist was distributed, latecomers—the poor and the slaves who had to work later—often were forced to go hungry because greedier fellow Christians had gobbled up the food, refusing to share and sometimes even getting drunk. Most scandalous, the leader of the congregation was openly living in an incestuous relationship, which shocked even the easygoing Corinthians.

Timothy made a few hesitant efforts to straighten out the situation in the Corinthian church. The coarse Corinthians, however, merely laughed. Timothy grew flustered. The rowdy church members began to tease him. Timothy smarted under their wisecracks about his youthful appearance, his blushing timidity. Nervously, he tried to speak to the ringleaders in the various factions, but he got nowhere. Timothy retreated.

Paul tried to inject some iron in the boy's will, and fired off a letter to the sarcastic Corinthian churchmen, pleading with them not to chill the enthusiasm of the hesitant lad nor to criticize his efforts too harshly. Paul, the experienced senior pastor, knew how easy it is to quench a youngster's enthusiasm with contempt, twisting him into a cynic.

Timothy, however, had become nothing but a joke to the Corinthian Christians. He tried to cope with the disorders, but everytime he started to assert his authority, he found himself in conflict. Never a person with a stomach for a fight, Timothy gave up.

He had flubbed—and he knew it. Timothy had blown his big opportunity. Deeply depressed and ashamed, Timothy left Corinth. His mission had been a complete failure. Knowing how badly he had fumbled, Timothy dejectedly hooked up again with the rest of Paul's group. He wondered what Paul and the others would say. He felt like excess baggage. Would they want him to stay around? Would they still need him? Timothy anxiously wondered.

Most youth secretly feel a sense of failure. Like all persons, young people need to be needed. When not really needed, however, the sense of failure is exacerbated and deepened.

Today's technological culture, geared to the knowledge and skills of the highly educated, makes a youth feel like a surplus article. Many of today's young people, locked into an educational system for over two decades of their lives, find that they are unneeded youths until their mid-or-late twenties. This prolonged adolescence and postponed acceptance by society diminishes any sense of self-worth. Until a generation ago, children and young people were a necessary part of the economy, were needed in the family shop or farm. When a boy sensed he was needed to carry the water pail for the older men, and as a youth knew he was needed to pitch in during the haying and threshing, he gained some sense of accomplishment and acceptance. The failure feelings were reduced. Today's youth, frozen out of the job market and prevented from assuming any responsible adult role, have little sense of being needed.

Some of our society's most gifted and most promising youngsters, sensing that they are unneeded, become most obsessed with their own sense of failure. Speaking for many, Tom, the gifted, sensitive young schoolboy in *Tea and Sympathy,* magnifies his failures to the point where he even blames himself for his parents' divorce, telling the kindly wife of a teacher, "I was supposed to hold them together. That was how I happened to come into the world. It didn't work. That's a terrible thing, you know, to make a flop of the first job you've got in life."

Timothy, dismayed at his own nonsuccess at Corinth, expected to be rebuffed by Paul and the others on the missionary team. Instead, he heard Paul compassionately refer to him as "our brother" (2 Corinthians 1:1). Despising himself for his failure, Timothy received the encouragement he desperately needed from Paul. Painfully, he began to rebuild a sense of self-confidence and self-esteem.

A person usually lives up to—or down to—what others expect of him. Timothy, regarded as "our brother" by the others in the missionary band, knew the acceptance and security of the Church as a *family.* He lived up to the title of *brother.*

In a culture which regards man as a commodity, we think of the worth of another human primarily in terms of whether or not he is successful. If he is successful, he is valuable; if not, he is worthless. Only the Church, inspired by the Christ who bestowed value on every human, can confer worth on another on the basis of what he *is,* not what he *does.* Only the family of those who know Christ's acceptance can free a person from the tyranny of scrambling frantically for success in order to prove one's value. In our society, life becomes a slave-market, in which one competes with others in auctioning off self-hood. It is no coincidence, however, that the word *worship* is actually the contraction of *worth-ship;* within the community of faith, we repeatedly restore worth-ship to one another. In response to Him who bestows the new status of *forgiven* failure on every person, we can take the risk of telling a fellow failure (and who is not?) that he is still *our brother.*